More Praise for
Why Be Happy When You Could Be Normal?

"Raucous . . . hums with a dark refulgence from its first pages . . .
[Winterson's] life with her adoptive parents was often
appalling, but it made her the writer she is."
—DWIGHT GARNER, *THE NEW YORK TIMES*

"[Winterson is] searingly honest yet effortlessly lithe as she slides
between forms, exuberant and unerring, demanding emotional
and intellectual expansion of herself and of us. . . .
In *Why Be Happy*, [Winterson's] emotional life is laid bare.
[Her] struggle to first accept and then love herself yields a bravely
frank narrative of truly coming undone."
—A. M. HOMES, *ELLE*

"[Winterson has] such a joy for life and love of language that she
quickly becomes her very own one-woman band—one that,
luckily for us, keeps playing on."
—LOUISA ERMELINO, *O, THE OPRAH MAGAZINE*

"Winterson writes with heartrending precision. . . .
Ferociously funny and unfathomably generous, Winterson's
exorcism-in-writing is an unforgettable quest for belonging."
—MEGAN O'GRADY, *VOGUE*

"Brave . . . As wide and bold an experiment in the memoir
form as any so far written. . . . *Why Be Happy* is proudly and sometimes
painfully honest. It is also, arguably, the finest and most
hopeful memoir to emerge in many years."
—JOHN BURNSIDE, *THE TIMES* (UK)

"It's a testament to Winterson's innate generosity,
as well as her talent, that she can showcase the outsize humor
her mother's equally capacious craziness provides even
as she reveals cruelties Mrs. Winterson imposed on her. . . .
To confront Mrs. Winterson head on, in life, in nonfiction, demands
courage; to survive requires imagination. . . . But put your money on
Jeanette Winterson. **Seventeen books ago, she proved
she had what she needed. Heroines are defined not
by their wounds, but by their triumphs.**"
—KATHRYN HARRISON, *THE NEW YORK TIMES BOOK REVIEW*

"Jeanette Winterson's sentences become lodged in the brain
for years, like song lyrics. . . . **Beautiful** . . . **Powerful** . . . **Shockingly
revealing** . . . Never has anyone so outsized and exceptional struggled
through such remembered pain to discover how intensely ordinary
she was meant to be."—JUNE THOMAS, SLATE

"That Winterson should have survived such a terrible early immersion
in darkness at all is a kind of miracle. That she should have emerged,
if not unscathed then still a functioning human being and
a creative artist, is an even greater accomplishment."
—MARTIN RUBIN, *SAN FRANCISCO CHRONICLE*

"There's always been something Byronic about Winterson—
a stormily passionate soul bitterly indicting the society that excludes her
while feeding on the Romantic drama of that exclusion. . . .
Why Be Happy **restores Winterson to her full power. . . .
This is a book that will inspire much underlining.**"
—LAURA MILLER, SALON

"[Winterson's] novels—mongrels of autobiography, myth, fantasy,
and formal experimentation—evince a colossal stamina for self-scrutiny.
. . . [A] proud and vivid portrait of working-class life . . .
**This bullet of a book is charged with risk, dark mirth,
hard-won self-knowledge. . . . You're in the hands of a master builder.**"
—PARUL SEHGAL, *BOOKFORUM*

"Offers literary surprises and flashes of magnificent generosity and humor."—VALERIE SAYERS, *THE WASHINGTON POST BOOK WORLD*

"Very possibly the most honest writing Winterson has ever done."
—NICOLA GRIFFITH, *LOS ANGELES REVIEW OF BOOKS*

"Raw . . . A highly unusual, scrupulously honest, and endearing memoir."—*PUBLISHERS WEEKLY* (STARRED REVIEW)

"Clarion, courageous, and vividly expressive, Winterson conducts a dramatic and revelatory inquiry into the forging of the self and liberating power of literature."—DONNA SEAMAN, *BOOKLIST* (STARRED)

"To read Jeanette Winterson's books is to know the exquisite torment of envying every bloody word she writes on the page."
—NICKI RICHESIN, *HUFFINGTON POST*

"Winterson pulls back the veil on her life as she really lived it and shows us that truth is not only stranger than fiction, but more painful and more beautiful as well. . . .
Winterson holds nothing back. . . . Written with poetic beauty."
—STEPHENIE HARRISON, *BOOKPAGE*

"Without her adoptive mother, [Winterson] might have been happy and normal, but she wouldn't have been Jeanette Winterson. Her childhood was ghastly, as bad as Dickens's stint in the blacking factory, but it was also the crucible for her incendiary talent."
—DAISY GOODWIN, *THE SUNDAY TIMES* (UK)

"An extraordinary tragicomic literary autobiography."
—MARK LAWSON, *THE GUARDIAN* (BEST BOOKS OF 2011)

"Searing . . . Winterson's truth is just as compelling as any fiction."
—*ENTERTAINMENT WEEKLY* (THE MUST LIST)

"Compelling . . . The specifics of [Winterson's] early abuse are vivid, violent, and no less horrifying for their familiarity. . . . If the memoir was begun as a final exorcism of the monster mother, it ends with a moving acceptance of her."—ARIFA AKBAR, *THE INDEPENDENT* (UK)

"Stunningly lovely and fearlessly reflective, *Why Be Happy* is a reminder of what the project of remembering and recording can—and should—be."—NORAH PIEHL, *BOOKREPORTER*

"**Essential . . . Wry, urgent . . . Doesn't miss a beat** . . . Winterson is frank about her own oddness, her fierceness. . . . If the first half of the book has been polished by retelling, the second half is raw, immediate. . . . Gone is the Nabokovian memoir in which the exquisite past is presented under glass, skewered by a pin. This is the age of instant communication, of forthright, unmediated responses. Winterson has her finger to the wind."—HERMIONE EYRE, *EVENING STANDARD*

"A detailed portrait of a life that saved itself . . . We are lucky she survived to tell the tale."—*LIBRARY JOURNAL* (STARRED REVIEW)

"The pages sing. . . . **A moving, artfully constructed piece of writing** that sustains tension until the last sentence."
—SARA WHEELER, *THE GLOBE AND MAIL*
(FAVORITE BOOK OF THE YEAR)

"Intense . . . [with] more charisma than a Pentecostal preacher . . .
A sad story, a funny story, a brave story."
—CHITRA RAMASWAMY, *THE SCOTSMAN*

"Recalls a feminine version of Edmund Gosse's *Father and Son* . . . Winterson lends all [her] fierce poetry, intelligence, and epigrammatic punch to [the] prose."—GEORDIE WILLIAMSON, *THE AUSTRALIAN*

"We are shown 'how it is when the mind works with its own brokenness,' and come to respect Winterson's psychological courage and her rage to love."—SHEENA JOUGHIN, *SUNDAY TELEGRAPH*

WHY BE HAPPY WHEN YOU COULD BE NORMAL?

Jeanette Winterson

Why Be Happy When You Could Be Normal?

GROVE PRESS
New York

First published in Great Britain in 2011 by Jonathan Cape
The Random House Group, London

Printed in the United States of America

ISBN: 978-0-8021-2087-8

eISBN: 978-0-8021-9475-6

Grove Press
an imprint of Grove/Atlantic, Inc.
154 West 14th Street
New York, NY 10011

Distributed by Publishers Group West

www.groveatlantic.com

14 15 16 17   10 9 8 7 6 5 4 3 2

To my three mothers:
Constance Winterson
Ruth Rendell
Ann S.

With love and thanks to Susie Orbach

Thanks as well to Paul Shearer who traced the family tree.
To Beeban Kidron's helpline! To Vicky Licorish and
the kids: my family. To all my friends who stood by me.
To Caroline Michel – fantastic agent and fabulous friend.
Everyone at Grove for backing this book: Morgan Entrekin,
Elisabeth Schmitz, Deb Seager and Jodie Hockensmith.
And to Heather Schroder at ICM and to A.M. Homes.

CONTENTS

1

The Wrong Crib

WHEN MY MOTHER WAS ANGRY with me, which was often, she said, 'The Devil led us to the wrong crib.'

The image of Satan taking time off from the Cold War and McCarthyism to visit Manchester in 1960 – purpose of visit: to deceive Mrs Winterson – has a flamboyant theatricality to it. She was a flamboyant depressive; a woman who kept a revolver in the duster drawer, and the bullets in a tin of Pledge. A woman who stayed up all night baking cakes to avoid sleeping in the same bed as my father. A woman with a prolapse, a thyroid condition, an enlarged heart, an ulcerated leg that never healed, and two sets of false teeth – matt for everyday, and a pearlised set for 'best'.

I do not know why she didn't/couldn't have children. I know that she adopted me because she wanted a friend (she had none), and because I was like a flare sent out into the world – a way of saying that she was here – a kind of X Marks the Spot.

She hated being a nobody, and like all children, adopted or not, I have had to live out some of her unlived life. We do that for our parents – we don't really have any choice.

She was alive when my first novel, *Oranges Are Not the Only Fruit*, was published in 1985. It is semi-autobiographical, in that it tells the story of a young girl adopted by Pentecostal parents. The girl is supposed to grow up and be a missionary. Instead she falls in love with a woman. Disaster. The girl leaves home, gets herself to Oxford University, returns home to find her mother has built a broadcast radio and is beaming out the Gospel to the heathen. The mother has a handle – she's called 'Kindly Light'.

The novel begins: '*Like most people I lived for a long time with my mother and father. My father liked to watch the wrestling, my mother liked to wrestle.*'

For most of my life I've been a bare-knuckle fighter. The one who wins is the one who hits the hardest. I was beaten as a child and I learned early never to cry. If I was locked out overnight I sat on the doorstep till the milkman came, drank both pints, left the empty bottles to enrage my mother, and walked to school.

We always walked. We had no car and no bus money. For me, the average was five miles a day: two miles for the round trip to school; three miles for the round trip to church.

Church was every night except Thursdays.

I wrote about some of these things in *Oranges*, and when it was published, my mother sent me a furious note in her immaculate copperplate handwriting demanding a phone call.

We hadn't seen each other for several years. I had left Oxford, was scraping together a life, and had written *Oranges* young – I was twenty-five when it was published.

I went to a phone box – I had no phone. She went to a phone box – she had no phone.

I dialled the Accrington code and number as

instructed, and there she was – who needs Skype? I could see her through her voice, her form solidifying in front of me as she talked.

She was a big woman, tallish and weighing around twenty stone. Surgical stockings, flat sandals, a Crimplene dress and a nylon headscarf. She would have done her face powder (keep yourself nice), but not lipstick (fast and loose).

She filled the phone box. She was out of scale, larger than life. She was like a fairy story where size is approximate and unstable. She loomed up. She expanded. Only later, much later, too late, did I understand how small she was to herself. The baby nobody picked up. The uncarried child still inside her.

But that day she was borne up on the shoulders of her own outrage. She said, 'It's the first time I've had to order a book in a false name.'

I tried to explain what I had hoped to do. I am an ambitious writer – I don't see the point of being anything; no, not anything at all, if you have no ambition for it. 1985 wasn't the day of the memoir – and in any case, I wasn't writing one. I was trying to get away from the received idea that women always write about 'experience' – the compass of what they know – while men write wide and bold – the big canvas, the experiment with form. Henry James misunderstood Jane Austen's comment that she wrote on small pieces of ivory – i.e. tiny observant minutiae. Much the same was said of Emily Dickinson and Virginia Woolf. Those things made me angry. In any case, why could there not be experience *and* experiment? Why could there not be the observed and the imagined? Why should a woman be limited by anything or anybody? Why should a woman not be ambitious for literature? Ambitious for herself?

Mrs Winterson was having none of it. She knew full well that writers were sex-crazed bohemians who broke the rules and didn't go out to work. Books had been forbidden in our house – I'll explain why later – and so for me to have written one, and had it published, and had it win a prize . . . and be standing in a phone box giving her a lecture on literature, a polemic on feminism . . .

The pips – more money in the slot – and I'm thinking, as her voice goes in and out like the sea, 'Why aren't you proud of me?'

The pips – more money in the slot – and I'm locked out and sitting on the doorstep again. It's really cold and I've got a newspaper under my bum and I'm huddled in my duffel coat.

A woman comes by and I know her. She gives me a bag of chips. She knows what my mother is like.

Inside our house the light is on. Dad's on the night shift, so she can go to bed, but she won't sleep. She'll read the Bible all night, and when Dad comes home, he'll let me in, and he'll say nothing, and she'll say nothing, and we'll act like it's normal to leave your kid outside all night, and normal never to sleep with your husband. And normal to have two sets of false teeth, and a revolver in the duster drawer . . .

We're still on the phone in our phone boxes. She tells me that my success is from the Devil, keeper of the wrong crib. She confronts me with the fact that I have used my own name in the novel – if it is a story, why is the main character called Jeanette?

Why?

I can't remember a time when I wasn't setting my story against hers. It was my survival from the very beginning. Adopted children are self-invented because we have to be; there is an absence, a void, a question mark at the very beginning of our lives. A crucial part of our story is gone, and violently, like a bomb in the womb.

The baby explodes into an unknown world that is only knowable through some kind of a story – of course that is how we all live, it's the narrative of our lives, but adoption drops you into the story after it has started. It's like reading a book with the first few pages missing. It's like arriving after curtain up. The feeling that something is missing never, ever leaves you – and it can't, and it shouldn't, because something *is* missing.

That isn't of its nature negative. The missing part, the missing past, can be an opening, not a void. It can be an entry as well as an exit. It is the fossil record, the imprint of another life, and although you can never have that life, your fingers trace the space where it might have been, and your fingers learn a kind of Braille.

There are markings here, raised like welts. Read them. Read the hurt. Rewrite them. Rewrite the hurt.

It's why I am a writer – I don't say 'decided' to be, or 'became'. It was not an act of will or even a conscious choice. To avoid the narrow mesh of Mrs Winterson's story I had to be able to tell my own.

Part fact part fiction is what life is. And it is always a cover story. I wrote my way out.

She said, 'But it's not true . . .'

Truth? This was a woman who explained the flash-dash of mice activity in the kitchen as ectoplasm.

There was a terraced house in Accrington, in Lancashire – we called those houses two-up two-down: two rooms downstairs, two rooms upstairs. Three of us lived together in that house for sixteen years. I told my version – faithful and invented, accurate and misremembered, shuffled in time. I told myself as hero like any shipwreck story. It was a shipwreck, and me thrown on the coastline of humankind, and finding it not altogether human, and rarely kind.

And I suppose that the saddest thing for me, thinking about the cover version that is *Oranges*, is that I wrote a story I could live with. The other one was too painful. I could not survive it.

I am often asked, in a tick-box kind of way, what is 'true' and what is not 'true' in *Oranges*. Did I work in a funeral parlour? Did I drive an ice-cream van? Did we have a Gospel Tent? Did Mrs Winterson build her own CB radio? Did she really stun tomcats with a catapult?

I can't answer these questions. I can say that there is a character in *Oranges* called Testifying Elsie who looks after the little Jeanette and acts as a soft wall against the hurt(ling) force of Mother.

I wrote her in because I couldn't bear to leave her out. I wrote her in because I really wished it had been that way. When you are a solitary child you find an imaginary friend.

There was no Elsie. There was no one like Elsie. Things were much lonelier than that.

I spent most of my school years sitting on the railings outside the school gates in the breaks. I was not a popular or a likeable child; too spiky, too angry, too intense, too odd. The churchgoing didn't encourage school friends, and school situations always pick out the misfit. Embroidering THE SUMMER IS ENDED AND WE ARE NOT YET SAVED on my gym bag made me easy to spot.

But even when I did make friends I made sure it went wrong . . .

If someone liked me, I waited until she was off guard, and then I told her I didn't want to be her friend any more. I watched the confusion and upset. The tears. Then I ran off, triumphantly in control, and very fast the triumph and the control leaked away, and then I cried and cried, because I had put myself on the outside again, on the doorstep again, where I didn't want to be.

Adoption is outside. You act out what it feels like to be the one who doesn't belong. And you act it out by trying to do to others what has been done to you. It is impossible to believe that anyone loves you for yourself.

I never believed that my parents loved me. I tried to love them but it didn't work. It has taken me a long time to learn how to love – both the giving and the receiving. I have written about love obsessively, forensically, and I know/knew it as the highest value.

I loved God of course, in the early days, and God loved me. That was something. And I loved animals and nature. And poetry. People were the problem. How do you love another person? How do you trust another person to love you?

I had no idea.

I thought that love was loss.

Why is the measure of love loss?

That was the opening line of a novel of mine – *Written on the Body* (1992). I was stalking love, trapping love, losing love, longing for love . . .

Truth for anyone is a very complex thing. For a writer, what you leave out says as much as those things you include. What lies beyond the margin of the text? The photographer frames the shot; writers frame their world.

Mrs Winterson objected to what I had put in, but it seemed to me that what I had left out was the story's silent twin. There are so many things that we can't say, because they are too painful. We hope that the things we can say will soothe the rest, or appease it in some way. Stories are compensatory. The world is unfair, unjust, unknowable, out of control.

When we tell a story we exercise control, but in such a way as to leave a gap, an opening. It is a version, but never the final one. And perhaps we hope that the silences will be heard by someone else, and the story can continue, can be retold.

When we write we offer the silence as much as the story. Words are the part of silence that can be spoken.

★

Mrs Winterson would have preferred it if I had been silent.

Do you remember the story of Philomel who is raped and then has her tongue ripped out by the rapist so that she can never tell?

I believe in fiction and the power of stories because that way we speak in tongues. We are not silenced. All of us, when in deep trauma, find we hesitate, we stammer; there are long pauses in our speech. The thing is stuck. We get our language back through the language of others. We can turn to the poem. We can open the book. Somebody has been there for us and deep-dived the words.

I needed words because unhappy families are conspiracies of silence. The one who breaks the silence is never forgiven. He or she has to learn to forgive him or herself.

God is forgiveness – or so that particular story goes, but in our house God was Old Testament and there was no forgiveness without a great deal of sacrifice. Mrs Winterson was unhappy and we had to be unhappy with her. She was waiting for the Apocalypse.

Her favourite song was 'God Has Blotted Them Out', which was meant to be about sins, but really was about anyone who had ever annoyed her, which was everyone. She just didn't like anyone and she just didn't like life. Life was a burden to be carried as far as the grave and then dumped. Life was a Vale of Tears. Life was a pre-death experience.

Every day Mrs Winterson prayed, 'Lord, let me die.' This was hard on me and my dad.

Her own mother had been a genteel woman who

had married a seductive thug, given him her money, and watched him womanise it away. For a while, from when I was about three, until I was about five, we had to live with my grandad, so that Mrs Winterson could nurse her mother, who was dying of throat cancer.

Although Mrs W was deeply religious, she believed in spirits, and it made her very angry that Grandad's girlfriend, as well as being an ageing barmaid with dyed blonde hair, was a medium who held seances in our very own front room.

After the seances my mother complained that the house was full of men in uniform from the war. When I went into the kitchen to get at the corned beef sandwiches I was told not to eat until the Dead had gone. This could take several hours, which is hard when you are four.

I took to wandering up and down the street asking for food. Mrs Winterson came after me and that was the first time I heard the dark story of the Devil and the crib . . .

In the crib next to me had been a little boy called Paul. He was my ghostly brother because his sainted self was always invoked when I was naughty. Paul would never have dropped his new doll into the pond (we didn't go near the surreal possibilities of Paul having been given a doll in the first place). Paul would not have filled his poodle pyjama case with tomatoes so that he could perform a stomach oper-ation with blood-like squish. Paul would not have hidden Grandad's gas mask (for some reason Grandad still had his wartime gas mask and I loved it). Paul would not have turned up at a nice birthday party, to which he had not been invited, wearing Grandad's gas mask.

If they had taken Paul instead of me, it would have been different, better. I was supposed to be a pal . . . like she had been to her mother.

And then her mother died and she shut herself up in her grief. I shut myself up in the larder because I had learned how to use the little key that opened the tins of corned beef.

I have a memory – true or not true?

The memory is surrounded by roses, which is odd because it is a violent and upsetting memory, but my grandad was a keen gardener and he particularly loved roses. I liked finding him, shirtsleeves rolled up, wearing a knitted waistcoat and spraying the blooms with water from a polished copper can with a piston pressure valve. He liked me, in an odd sort of way, and he disliked my mother, and she hated him – not in an angry way, but with a toxic submissive resentment.

I am wearing my favourite outfit – a cowboy suit and a fringed hat. My small body is slung from side to side with cap-gun Colts.

A woman comes into the garden and Grandad tells me to go inside and find my mother who is making her usual pile of sandwiches.

I run in – Mrs Winterson takes off her apron and goes to answer the door.

I am peeping from down the hallway. There is an argument between the two women, a terrible argument that I can't understand, and something fierce and frightening, like animal fear. Mrs Winterson slams the door and leans on it for a second. I creep out of my peeping place. She turns around. There I am in my cowboy outfit.

'Was that my mum?'

Mrs Winterson hits me and the blow knocks me back. Then she runs upstairs.

I go out into the garden. Grandad is spraying the roses. He ignores me. There is no one there.

2

My Advice To
Anybody Is: Get Born

I WAS BORN IN MANCHESTER in 1959. It was a good
place to be born.

Manchester is in the south of the north of England.

Its spirit has a contrariness in it – a south and north
bound up together – at once untamed and unmetro-
politan; at the same time, connected and worldly.

Manchester was the world's first industrial city; its
looms and mills transforming itself and the fortunes
of Britain. Manchester had canals, easy access to the
great port of Liverpool, and railways that carried
thinkers and doers up and down to London. Its influ-
ence affected the whole world.

Manchester was all mix. It was radical – Marx and
Engels were here. It was repressive – the Peterloo
Massacres and the Corn Laws. Manchester spun riches
beyond anybody's wildest dreams, and wove despair
and degradation into the human fabric. It was
Utilitarian, in that everything was put to the test of
'Does this work?' It was Utopian – its Quakerism, its
feminism, its anti-slavery movement, its socialism, its
communism.

The Manchester mix of alchemy and geography
can't be separated. What it is, where it is . . . long
before the Romans had a fort here in AD 79, the
Celts worshipped the river goddess of the Medlock.

13

This was Mam-ceaster – and Mam is mother, is breast, life force . . . energy.

To the south of Manchester is the Cheshire plain. Human settlements in Cheshire are among the earliest to be found in the British Isles. There were villages here, and strange yet direct routes to what became Liverpool on the vast and deep River Mersey.

To the north and east of Manchester are the Pennines – the wild rough low mountain range that runs through the north of England, where early settlements were scattered and few, and where men and women lived solitary, often fugitive lives. The smooth Cheshire plain, civilised and settled, and the rough tussocky Lancashire Pennines, the brooding place, the escaping place.

Until the boundary changes, Manchester was partly in Lancashire and partly in Cheshire – making it a double city rooted in restless energy and contradictions.

The textile boom of the early nineteenth century sucked all the surrounding villages and satellite settlements into one vast moneymaking machine. Until the First World War, 65 per cent of the world's cotton was processed in Manchester. Its nickname was Cottonopolis.

Imagine it – the vast steamed-powered gaslit factories and the back-to back tenements thrown up in between. The filth, the smoke, the stink of dye and ammonia, sulphur and coal. The cash, the ceaseless activity day and night, the deafening noise of looms, of trains, of trams, of wagons on cobbles, of teeming relentless human life, a Niebelheim hell, and a triumphant work of labour and determination.

Everyone who visited Manchester both admired it

and felt appalled. Charles Dickens used it as the basis for his novel *Hard Times*; the best of times and the worst of times were here – everything the machine could achieve, and the terrible human cost.

Men and women, ill-clad, exhausted, drunken and sickly, worked twelve-hour shifts six days a week, went deaf, clogged their lungs, saw no daylight, took their children to crawl under the terrifying clatter of the working looms, picking up fluff, sweeping, losing hands, arms, legs, small children, weak children, uneducated and often unwanted, the women working as hard as the men, and they also bore the burden of the house.

> A horde of ragged women and children, as filthy as the swine that thrive upon the garbage heaps and puddles – neither drains nor pavements – standing pools in all directions – the dark smoke of a dozen factory chimneys . . . a measureless filth and stench.
>
> Engels, *The Condition of the English Working Class in England* (1844)

The rawness of Manchester life, where nothing could be hidden out of sight, where the successes and the shames of this new uncontrollable reality were everywhere, pitched Manchester into a radicalism that became more important in the long run than its cotton trade.

Manchester was *active*. The Pankhurst family had had enough of all talk and no vote, and in 1903 went militant with the Women's Social and Political Union.

15

The first Trades Union Conference was held in Manchester in 1868. Its purpose was change, not talk about change.

Twenty years earlier, in 1848, Karl Marx had published *The Communist Manifesto* – much of it written out of his time in Manchester with his friend Friedrich Engels. The men were theorists made activists by their time in a city that had no time for thinking, that was all the frenzy of doing – and Marx wanted to turn that fiendish unstoppable energy of doing into something good . . .

Engels' time in Manchester, working for his father's firm, opened up to him the brutal reality of working-class life. *The Condition of the Working Class in England* is still worth reading – a frightening, upsetting account of the effects of the Industrial Revolution on ordinary people – what happens when people 'regard each other only as useful objects'.

Where you are born – what you are born into, the place, the history of the place, how that history mates with your own – stamps who you are, whatever the pundits of globalisation have to say. My birth mother worked as a machinist in a factory. My adoptive father laboured as a road mender, then shovelled coal at the power station on shift work. He worked ten hours at a stretch, did overtime when he could, saved the bus fare by biking six miles each way, and never had enough money for meat more than twice a week or anything more exotic than one week a year at the seaside.

He was no better off and no worse off than anyone else we knew. We were the working class. We were the mass at the factory gates.

16

I didn't want to be in the teeming mass of the working class. I wanted to work, but not like him. I didn't want to disappear. I didn't want to live and die in the same place with only a week at the seaside in between. I dreamed of escape – but what is terrible about industrialisation is that it makes escape necessary. In a system that generates masses, individualism is the only way out. But then what happens to community – to society?

As Prime Minister Margaret Thatcher said, in the spirit of her friend Ronald Reagan, celebrating the Me decade of the 1980s, 'There is no such thing as society . . .'

But I didn't care about any of that when I was growing up – and I didn't understand it either.

I just wanted to get out.

My birth mother, they told me, was a little red thing from out of the Lancashire looms, who at seventeen gave birth to me, easy as a cat.

She came from the village of Blakely where Queen Victoria had her wedding dress made, though by the time my mother was born and I was born, Blakely was a village no longer. The country forced into the city – that is the story of industrialisation, and it has a despair in it, and an excitement in it, and a brutality in it, and poetry in it, and all of those things are in me.

When I was born the looms had gone but not the long low terraces of houses sometimes stone sometimes brick under shallow-pitched roofs of slate tiles. With slate roof tiles your pitch can be as shallow as 33 degrees – with stone tiles you must allow 45 degrees or even 54. The look of a place was all to do with the materials to hand. Steeper roofs of stone tiles coax the water to run slower as it bumps over the rises and indentations of the stone. Slate is fast and flat, and if slate roofs are too steep, the water waterfalls straight over the gutters. The flow is slowed by the pitch.

That typical flat grey unlovely look of the northern industrial roofscape is no-nonsense efficient, like the industry the houses were built to support. You get on with it, you work hard, you don't try for beauty or dreaming. You don't build for the view. Thick flagstone floors, small mean rooms, dismal backyards.

If you do climb to the top of the house, all there is are the squat stacks of the shared chimneys, smoking coal into the haze that somewhere hides the sky.

But . . .

The Lancashire Pennines are the dreaming place. Low, thick-chested, massy, hard, the ridge of hills is always visible, like a rough watcher who loves something he can't defend, but stays anyway, hunched over the ugliness human beings make. Stays scarred and battered but stays.

If you drive along the M62 from Manchester towards Accrington where I was brought up, you will see the Pennines, shocking in their suddenness and their silence. This is a landscape of few words, taciturn, reluctant. It is not an easy beauty.

But it is beautiful.

Sometime, between six weeks and six months old, I got picked up from Manchester and taken to

Accrington. It was all over for me and the woman whose baby I was.

She was gone. I was gone.

I was adopted.

21 January 1960 is the date when John William Winterson, Labourer, and Constance Winterson, Clerk, got the baby they thought they wanted and took it home to 200 Water Street, Accrington, Lancashire.

They had bought the house for £200 in 1947.

1947, the coldest British winter of the twentieth century, snow so high it reached the top of the upright piano as they pushed it in through the door.

1947, and the war ended, and my dad out of the army, doing his best, trying to make a living, and his wife throwing her wedding ring in the gutter and refusing all sexual relations.

I don't know, and never will, whether she couldn't have children or whether she just wouldn't put herself through the necessaries.

I know they both drank a bit and they both smoked before they found Jesus. And I don't think my mother was depressed in those days. After the tent crusade, where they became Pentecostal evangelical Christians, they both gave up drink — except for cherry brandy at New Year — and my father traded his Woodbines for Polo mints. My mother carried on smoking because she said it kept her weight down. Her smoking had to be a secret though, and she kept an air freshener she claimed was fly spray in her handbag.

No one seemed to think it was unusual to keep fly spray in your handbag.

She was convinced that God would find her a child,

and I suppose that if God is providing the baby, having sex can be crossed off the list. I don't know how Dad felt about this. Mrs Winterson always said, 'He's not like other men . . .'

Every Friday he gave her his pay packet and she gave him back enough change for three packets of Polo mints.

She said, 'They're his only pleasure . . .'

Poor Dad.

When he got married again at seventy-two, his new wife Lillian, who was ten years younger and a good-time girl, told me it was like sleeping with a red-hot poker.

Until I was two years old, I screamed. This was evidence in plain sight that I was possessed by the Devil. Child psychology hadn't reached Accrington, and in spite of important work by Winnicott, Bowlby and Balint on attachment, and the trauma of early separation from the love object that is the mother, a screaming baby wasn't a broken-hearted baby – she was a Devil baby.

That gave me a strange power as well as all the vulnerabilities. I think my new parents were frightened of me.

Babies are frightening – raw tyrants whose only kingdom is their own body. My new mother had a lot of problems with the body – her own, my dad's, their bodies together, and mine. She had muffled her own body in flesh and clothes, suppressed its appetites with a fearful mix of nicotine and Jesus, dosed it with purgatives that made her vomit, submitted it to doctors, who administered enemas and pelvic rings, subdued its desires for ordinary touch and comfort, and suddenly, not out of her own body, and with no preparation, she had a thing that was all body.

A burping, spraying, sprawling faecal thing blasting the house with rude life.

She was thirty-seven when I arrived, and my dad was forty. That is pretty normal these days, but it wasn't normal in the 1960s when people married early and started their families in their twenties. She and my father had already been married for fifteen years.

They had an old-fashioned marriage in that my father never cooked, and when I arrived, my mother never worked outside the home. This was very bad for her, and turned her inward-looking nature into walled-in depression. There were many fights, and about many things, but the battle between us was really the battle between happiness and unhappiness.

I was very often full of rage and despair. I was always lonely. In spite of all that I was and am in love with life. When I was upset I went roaming into the Pennines – all day on a jam sandwich and a bottle of milk. When I was locked outside, or the other favourite, locked in the coal-hole, I made up stories and forgot about the cold and the dark. I know these are ways of surviving, but maybe a refusal, any refusal, to be broken lets in enough light and air to keep believing in the world – the dream of escape.

I found some papers of mine recently, with the usual teenage poetic dross, but also a line I unconsciously used later in *Oranges* – 'What I want does exist if I dare to find it . . .'

Yes, it's a young person's melodrama, but that attitude seems to have had a protective function.

I liked best the stories about buried treasure and lost children and locked-up princesses. That the treasure is found, the children returned and the princesses freed, seemed hopeful to me.

And the Bible told me that even if nobody loved me on earth, there was God in heaven who loved me like I was the only one who had ever mattered.

I believed that. It helped me.

My mother, Mrs Winterson, didn't love life. She didn't believe that anything would make life better. She once told me that the universe is a cosmic dustbin – and after I had thought about this for a bit, I asked her if the lid was on or off.

'On,' she said. 'Nobody escapes.'

The only escape was Armageddon – the last battle when heaven and earth will be rolled up like a scroll, and the saved get to live in eternity with Jesus.

She still had her War Cupboard. Every week she put another tin in there – some of the tins had been in there since 1947 – and I think that when the last battle started we were meant to live under the stairs with the shoe polish and eat our way through the tins. My earlier successes with the corned beef gave me no cause for further alarm. We would eat our rations and wait for Jesus.

I wondered if we would be personally liberated by Jesus himself, but Mrs Winterson thought not. 'He'll send an angel.'

So that would be it – an angel under the stairs.

I wondered where the wings would fit, but Mrs Winterson said the angel would not actually join us under the stairs – only open the door and tell us it was time to come out. Our mansion in the sky was ready.

Those elaborate interpretations of a post-apocalypse future occupied her mind. Sometimes she seemed happy, and played the piano, but unhappiness was always close by, and some other thought would cloud her mind so that she stopped playing, abruptly, and closed the lid, and walked up and down, up and down the back alley under the lines of strung washing, walking, walking as though she had lost something.

She had lost something. It was a big something. She had lost/was losing life.

We were matched in our lost and losing. I had lost the warm safe place, however chaotic, of the first person I loved. I had lost my name and my identity. Adopted children are dislodged. My mother felt that the whole of life was a grand dislodgement. We both wanted to go Home.

Still, I was excited about the Apocalypse because Mrs Winterson made it exciting, but I secretly hoped that life would go on until I could be grown up and find out more about it.

The one good thing about being shut in a coal-hole is that it prompts reflection.

Read on its own that is an absurd sentence. But as I try and understand how life works – and why some people cope better than others with adversity – I come back to something to do with saying yes to life, which is love of life, however inadequate, and love for the self, however found. Not in the me-first way that is the opposite of life and love, but with a salmon-like determination to swim upstream, however choppy upstream is, because this is your stream . . .

Which brings me back to happiness, and a quick look at the word.

Our primary meaning now is the feeling of pleasure and contentment; a buzz, a zestiness, the tummy upwards feel of good and right and relaxed and alive . . . you know . . .

But earlier meanings build in the *hap* – in Middle English, that is 'happ', in Old English, 'gehapp' – the chance or fortune, good or bad, that falls to you. Hap is your lot in life, the hand you are given to play.

How you meet your 'hap' will determine whether or not you can be 'happy'.

What the Americans, in their constitution, call 'the right to the pursuit of happiness' (please note, not 'the right to happiness'), is the right to swim upstream, salmon-wise.

Pursuing happiness, and I did, and I still do, is not at all the same as being happy – which I think is fleeting, dependent on circumstances, and a bit bovine.

If the sun is shining, stand in it – yes, yes, yes. Happy times are great, but happy times pass – they have to – because time passes.

The pursuit of happiness is more elusive; it is life-long, and it is not goal-centred.

What you are pursuing is meaning – a meaningful life. There's the *hap* – the fate, the draw that is yours, and it isn't fixed, but changing the course of the stream, or dealing new cards, whatever metaphor you want to use – that's going to take a lot of energy. There are times when it will go so wrong that you will barely be alive, and times when you realise that being barely alive, on your own terms, is better than living a bloated half-life on someone else's terms.

The pursuit isn't all or nothing – it's all AND nothing. Like all Quest Stories.

When I was born I became the visible corner of a folded map.

The map has more than one route. More than one destination. The map that is the unfolding self is not exactly leading anywhere. The arrow that says YOU ARE HERE is your first coordinate. There is a lot that you can't change when you are a kid. But you can pack for the journey . . .

3

In The Beginning Was The Word

My mother had taught me to read from the Book of Deuteronomy because it is full of animals (mostly unclean). Whenever we read 'Thou shall not eat any beast that does not chew the cud or part the hoof' she drew all the creatures mentioned. Horses, bunnies and little ducks were vague fabulous things, but I knew all about pelicans, rock badgers, sloths and bats . . . My mother drew winged insects, and the birds of the air, but my favourite ones were the seabed ones, the molluscs. I had a fine collection from the beach at Blackpool. She had a blue pen for the waves and brown ink for the scaly-backed crab. Lobsters were red biro . . . Deuteronomy had its drawbacks; it is full of Abominations and Unmentionables. Whenever we read about a bastard, or someone with crushed testicles, my mother turned over the page and said, 'Leave that to the Lord,' but when she'd gone, I'd sneak a look. I was glad I didn't have testicles. They sounded like intestines, only on the outside, and the men in the Bible were always having them cut off and not being able to go to church. Horrid.

from *Oranges Are Not the Only Fruit*

M Y MOTHER WAS IN CHARGE of language. My father had never really learned to read — he could manage slowly, with his finger on the line, but he had left school at twelve and gone to work at the Liverpool docks. Before he was twelve, no one had bothered to read to him. His own father had been a drunk who often took his small son to the pub with him, left him outside, staggered out hours later and walked home, and forgot my dad, asleep in a doorway.

Dad loved Mrs Winterson reading out loud — and I did too. She always stood up while we two sat down, and it was intimate and impressive all at the same time.

She read the Bible every night for half an hour, starting at the beginning, and making her way through all sixty-six books of the Old and New Testaments. When she got to her favourite bit, the Book of Revelation, and the Apocalypse, and everyone being exploded and the Devil in the bottomless pit, she gave us all a week off to think about things. Then she started again, Genesis Chapter One. *In the beginning God created the heavens and the earth . . .*

It seemed to me to be a lot of work to make a whole planet, a whole universe, and blow it up, but that is one of the problems with the literal-minded versions of Christianity; why look after the planet when you know it is all going to end in pieces?

My mother was a good reader, confident and dramatic. She read the Bible as though it had just been written — and perhaps it was like that for her. I got a sense early on that the power of a text is not time-bound. The words go on doing their work.

Working-class families in the north of England used to hear the 1611 Bible regularly at church and at home, and as there was still a 'thee' and 'thou' or 'tha' in daily speech for us, the language didn't seem too difficult. I especially liked 'the quick and the dead' – you really get a feel for the difference if you live in a house with mice and a mousetrap.

In the 1960s many men – and they were men not women – attended evening classes at the Working Men's Institutes or the Mechanics' Institute – another progressive initiative coming out of Manchester. The idea of 'bettering' yourself was not seen as elitist then, neither was it assumed that all values are relative, nor that all culture is more or less identical – whether Hammer Horror or Shakespeare.

Those evening classes were big on Shakespeare – and none of the men ever complained that the language was difficult. Why not? It wasn't difficult – it was the language of the 1611 Bible; the King James Version appeared in the same year as the first advertised performance of *The Tempest*. Shakespeare wrote *The Winter's Tale* that year.

It was a useful continuity, destroyed by the well-meaning, well-educated types who didn't think of the consequences for the wider culture to have modern Bibles with the language stripped out. The consequence was that uneducated men and women, men like my father, and kids like me in ordinary schools, had no more easy everyday connection to four hundred years of the English language.

A lot of older people I knew, my parents' generation, quoted Shakespeare and the Bible and sometimes the metaphysical poets like John Donne, without knowing the source, or misquoting and mixing.

My mother, being apocalyptic by nature, liked to

greet any news of either calamity or good fortune with the line 'Ask not for whom the bell tolls . . .' This was delivered in a suitably sepulchral tone. As evangelical churches don't have any bells, I never understood, even, that it was about death, and certainly not till I got to Oxford did I find it was a misquote from a prose passage of John Donne, the one that begins 'No man is an island entire of itself . . .' and that ends 'never send to know for whom the bell tolls . . .'

Once, my dad won the works raffle. He came home very pleased with himself. My mother asked him what was the prize?

'Fifty pounds and two boxes of Wagon Wheels.' (These were large and horrible chocolate-style biscuits with a wagon and a cowboy on the wrapper.)

My mother did not reply, so my dad pressed on. 'That's good, Connie – are you glad?'

She said, 'Ask not for whom the bell tolls . . .'

So we didn't.

She had other favourite lines. Our gas oven blew up. The repairman came out and said he didn't like the look of it, which was unsurprising as the oven and the wall were black. Mrs Winterson replied, 'It's a fault to heaven, a fault against the dead, and a fault to nature.' That is a heavy load for a gas oven to bear.

She liked that phrase and it was more than once used towards me; when some well-wisher asked how I was, Mrs W looked down and sighed, 'She's a fault to heaven, a fault against the dead, and a fault to nature.'

This was even worse for me than it had been for the gas oven. I was particularly worried about the 'dead' part, and wondered which buried and unfortunate relative I had so offended.

Later, I found the lines in *Hamlet*.

A general phrase, for her and others, when making an unfavourable comparison, was to say, 'As a crab's like an apple.'

That is the Fool in *King Lear*. Yet it has a northern ring to it, partly I think because a working-class tradition is an oral tradition, not a bookish one, but its richness of language comes from absorbing some of the classics in school – they all learned by rote – and by creatively using language to tell a good story. I think back and I realise that our stock of words was not small – and we loved images.

Until the eighties, visual culture, TV culture, mass culture, had not made much of an impact up north – there was still a strong local culture and a powerful dialect. I left in 1979, and it was not that much different from 1959. By 1990, when we went back to film *Oranges* for the BBC, it was totally different.

For the people I knew, books were few and stories were everywhere, and how you tell 'em was everything. Even an exchange on a bus had to have a narrative.

'They've no money so they're having their honeymoon in Morecambe.'

'That's a shame – there's nowt to do in Morecambe once you've had a swim.'

'I feel sorry for 'em.'

'Aye, but it's only a week's honeymoon – I know a woman who spent all her married life in Morecambe.'

Ask not for whom the bell tolls . . .

★

30

My mother told stories – of their life in the war and how she'd played the accordion in the air-raid shelter and it had got rid of the rats. Apparently rats like violins and pianos but they can't stand the accordion . . .

About her life sewing parachutes – all the girls stole the silk for clothes.

About her life to come, when she'd have a mansion and no neighbours. All she ever wanted was for everyone to go away. And when I did she never forgave me.

She loved miracle stories, probably because her life was as far away from a miracle as Jupiter is from the Earth. She believed in miracles, even though she never got one – well, maybe she did get one, but that was me, and she didn't know that miracles often come in disguise.

I was a miracle in that I could have taken her out of her life and into a life she would have liked a lot. It never happened, but that doesn't mean it wasn't there to happen. All of that has been a brutal lesson to me in not overlooking or misunderstanding what is actually there, in your hands, now. We always think the thing we need to transform everything – the miracle – is elsewhere, but often it is right next to us. Sometimes it is us, ourselves.

The miracle stories she loved were Bible ones, like the Five Loaves and Two Fishes, probably because we never had quite enough to eat, and ones from the front line of Jesus in the World.

I particularly liked the Hallelujah Giant – eight feet tall, shrunk to six feet three through the prayers of the faithful.

And there were the stories about bags of coal

31

appearing from nowhere, and an extra pound in your purse when you needed it most.

She didn't like stories about being raised from the dead. She always said that if she died we weren't to pray to bring her back.

Her funeral money was sewn into the curtains – at least it was until I stole it. When I unpicked the hem, there was note in her handwriting – she was so proud of her handwriting – it said: '*Don't cry Jack and Jeanette. You know where I am.*'

I did cry. Why is the measure of love loss?

4

The Trouble With A Book . . .

THERE WERE SIX BOOKS IN our house.
One was the Bible and two were commentaries
on the Bible. My mother was a pamphleteer by
temperament and she knew that sedition and contro-
versy are fired by printed matter. Ours was not a
secular house, and my mother was determined that I
should have no secular influences.

I asked my mother why we couldn't have books
and she said, 'The trouble with a book is that you
never know what's in it until it's too late.'

I thought to myself, 'Too late for what?'

I began to read books in secret – there was no
other way – and every time I opened the pages, I
wondered if this time it would be too late; a final
draught (draft) that would change me forever, like
Alice's bottle, like the tremendous potion in *Dr Jekyll
and Mr Hyde*, like the mysterious liquid that seals the
fate of Tristan and Isolde.

In myths, in legends, in fairy stories, and in all the
stories that borrow from these basics, both size and
shape are approximate, and subject to change. This
includes the size and shape of the heart, where the
beloved can suddenly be despised, or where the loathed
can become the loved. Look what happens in
Shakespeare's *A Midsummer Night's Dream* when Puck's
eyedrops turn Lysander from an opportunistic

womaniser into a devoted husband. In Shakespeare's use of the magic potion, it is not that the object of desire itself is altered – the women are who they are – rather that the man is forced to see them differently.

In the same play, Titania briefly falls for a clod wearing an ass's head – a mischievous use of the transforming potion, but one that questions reality: Do we see what we think we see? Do we love as we believe we love?

Growing up is difficult. Strangely, even when we have stopped growing physically, we seem to have to keep on growing emotionally, which involves both expansion and shrinkage, as some parts of us develop and others must be allowed to disappear . . . Rigidity never works; we end up being the wrong size for our world.

I used to have an anger so big it would fill up any house. I used to feel so hopeless that I was like Tom Thumb who has to hide under a chair so as not to be trodden on.

Do you remember how Sinbad tricks the genie? Sinbad opens the bottle and out comes a three-hundred-foot-tall genie who will kill poor Sinbad stone dead. So Sinbad appeals to his vanity and bets he can't get back in the bottle. As soon as the genie does so, Sinbad stoppers the neck until the genie learns better manners.

Jung, not Freud, liked fairy tales for what they tell us about human nature. Sometimes, often, a part of us is both volatile and powerful – the towering anger that can kill you and others, and that threatens to overwhelm everything. We can't negotiate with that powerful but enraged part of us until we teach it better manners – which means getting it back in the bottle to show who is really in charge. This isn't repression, but it is about finding a container. In therapy, the therapist acts as a container for what we daren't let out, because it is so scary, or what lets itself out every so often, and lays waste to our lives.

The fairy tales warn us that there is no such thing as standard size – that is an illusion of industrial life – an illusion farmers still struggle with when trying to supply uniform vegetables to supermarkets . . . no, size is both particular and subject to change.

The stories of the gods appearing in human form – scaled-down power deities – are also stories against judging by appearances – things are not what they seem.

It seems to me that being the right size for your world – and knowing that both you and your world are not by any means fixed dimensions – is a valuable clue to learning how to live.

Mrs Winterson was too big for her world, but she crouched gloomy and awkward under its low shelf, now and again exploding to her full three hundred feet, and towering over us. Then, because it was useless, redundant, only destructive, or so it seemed, she shrank back again, defeated.

I am short, so I like the little guy/underdog stories, but they are not straightforwardly about one size versus another. Think about, say, *Jack and the Beanstalk*, which is basically a big ugly stupid giant, and a smart little Jack who is fast on his feet. OK, but the unstable element is the beanstalk, which starts as a bean and grows into a huge tree-like thing that Jack climbs to reach the castle. This bridge between two worlds is unpredictable and very surprising. And later, when the giant tries to climb after Jack, the beanstalk has to be chopped down pronto. This suggests to me that the pursuit of happiness, which we may as well call life, is full of surprising temporary elements – we get somewhere we couldn't go otherwise and we profit from the trip, but we can't stay there, it isn't our world, and we shouldn't let that world come crashing down into the one we can inhabit. The beanstalk has to be chopped down. But the large-scale riches from the 'other world' can be brought into ours, just as Jack makes off with the singing harp and the golden hen. Whatever we 'win' will accommodate itself to our size and form – just as the miniature princesses and the frog princes all assume the true form necessary for their coming life, and ours.

Size does matter.

In my novel *Sexing the Cherry* (1989) I invented a character called the Dog Woman; a giantess who lives on the River Thames. She suffers because she is too big for her world. She was another reading of my mother.

Six books . . . my mother didn't want books falling into my hands. It never occurred to her that I fell into the books – that I put myself inside them for safe keeping.

Every week Mrs Winterson sent me to the Accrington Public Library to collect her stash of murder mysteries. Yes, that is a contradiction, but our contradictions are never so to ourselves. She liked Ellery Queen and

Raymond Chandler, and when I challenged her over the business of 'the trouble with a book [to rhyme with spook] is that you never know what's in it until it's too late . . .', she replied that if you know there is a body coming, it isn't so much of a shock.

I was allowed to read non-fiction books about kings and queens and history, but never, ever, fiction. Those were the books there was trouble in . . .

The Accrington Public Library was a fully stocked library built out of stone on the values of an age of self-help and betterment. It was finally finished in 1908 with money from the Carnegie Foundation. Outside were carved heads of Shakespeare and Milton, Chaucer and Dante. Inside were art nouveau tiles and a gigantic stained-glass window that said useful things like INDUSTRY AND PRUDENCE CONQUER.

The library held all the Eng lit classics, and quite a few surprises like Gertrude Stein. I had no idea of what to read or in what order, so I just started alphabetically. Thank God her last name was Austen . . .

At home one of the six books was unexpected; a copy of *Morte d'Arthur* by Thomas Mallory. It was a beautiful edition with pictures, and it had belonged to a bohemian, educated uncle – her mother's brother. So she kept it and I read it.

The stories of Arthur, of Lancelot and Guinevere, of Merlin, of Camelot and the Grail, docked into me like the missing molecule of a chemical compound.

I have gone on working with the Grail stories all my life. They are stories of loss, of loyalty, of failure, of recognition, of second chances. I used to have to put the book down and run past the part where Perceval, searching for the Grail, is given a vision of it one day, and then, because he is unable to ask the crucial question, the Grail disappears. Perceval spends twenty years wandering in the woods, looking for the thing that he found, that was given to him, that seemed so easy, that was not.

Later, when things were difficult for me with my work, and I felt that I had lost or turned away from something I couldn't even identify, it was the Perceval story that gave me hope. There might be a second chance . . .

In fact, there are more than two chances — many more. I know now, after fifty years, that the finding/ losing, forgetting/remembering, leaving/returning, never stops. The whole of life is about another chance, and while we are alive, till the very end, there is always another chance.

And of course I loved the Lancelot story because it is all about longing and unrequited love.

Yes, the stories are dangerous, she was right. A book is a magic carpet that flies you off elsewhere. A book is a door. You open it. You step through. Do you come back?

I was sixteen and my mother was about to throw me out of the house forever, for breaking a very big rule — even bigger than the forbidden books. The rule was not just No Sex, but definitely No Sex With Your Own Sex.

I was scared and unhappy.

I remember going down to the library to collect the murder mysteries. One of the books my mother had ordered was called *Murder in the Cathedral* by T. S. Eliot. She assumed it was a gory story about nasty monks – and she liked anything that was bad for the Pope.

The book looked a bit short to me – mysteries are usually quite long – so I had a look and saw that it was written in verse. Definitely not right . . . I had never heard of T. S. Eliot. I thought he might be related to George Eliot. The librarian told me he was an American poet who had lived in England for most of his life. He had died in 1964, and he had won the Nobel Prize.

I wasn't reading poetry because my aim was to work my way through ENGLISH LITERATURE IN PROSE A-Z.

But this was different . . .

I read: *This is one moment, / But know that another / Shall pierce you with a sudden painful joy.*

I started to cry.

Readers looked up reproachfully, and the librarian reprimanded me, because in those days you weren't even allowed to sneeze in a library, let alone weep. So I took the book outside and read it all the way through, sitting on the steps in the usual northern gale.

The unfamiliar and beautiful play made things bearable that day, and the things it made bearable were another failed family – the first one was not my fault but all adopted children blame themselves. The second failure was definitely my fault.

I was confused about sex and sexuality, and upset about the straightforward practical problems of where to live, what to eat, and how to do my A levels.

I had no one to help me, but the T. S. Eliot helped me.

So when people say that poetry is a luxury, or an option, or for the educated middle classes, or that it shouldn't be read at school because it is irrelevant, or any of the strange and stupid things that are said about poetry and its place in our lives, I suspect that the people doing the saying have had things pretty easy. A tough life needs a tough language – and that is what poetry is. That is what literature offers – a language powerful enough to say how it is.

It isn't a hiding place. It is a finding place.

In many ways it was time for me to go. The books had got the better of me, and my mother had got the better of the books.

I used to work on the market on Saturdays, and after school on Thursdays and Fridays, packing up. I used the money to buy books. I smuggled them inside and hid them under the mattress.

Anybody with a single bed, standard size, and a collection of paperbacks, standard size, will know that seventy-two per layer can be accommodated under the mattress. By degrees my bed began to rise visibly, like the Princess and the Pea, so that soon I was sleeping closer to the ceiling than to the floor.

My mother was suspicious-minded, but even if she had not been, it was clear that her daughter was going up in the world.

One night she came in and saw the corner of a paperback sticking out from under the mattress. She pulled it out and examined it with her flashlight. It was an unlucky choice; D. H. Lawrence, *Women in Love.*

Mrs Winterson knew that Lawrence was a satanist and a pornographer, and hurling it out of the window, she rummaged and rifled and I came tumbling off the bed while she threw book after book out of the window and into the backyard. I was grabbing books and trying to hide them, the dog was running off with them, my dad was standing helpless in his pyjamas.

When she had done, she picked up the little paraffin stove we used to heat the bathroom, went into the yard, poured paraffin over the books and set them on fire.

I watched them blaze and blaze and remember thinking how warm it was, how light, on the freezing Saturnian January night. And books have always been light and warmth to me.

I had bound them all in plastic because they were precious. Now they were gone.

In the morning there were stray bits of texts all over the yard and in the alley. Burnt jigsaws of books. I collected some of the scraps.

It is probably why I write as I do – collecting the scraps, uncertain of continuous narrative. What does Eliot say? *These fragments have I shored against my ruin* . . .

I was very quiet for a while, but I had realised something important: whatever is on the outside can be taken away at any time. Only what is inside you is safe.

I began to memorise text. We had always memorised long chunks of the Bible, and it seems that people in oral traditions have better memories than those who rely on stored text.

There was a time when record-keeping wasn't an act of administration; it was an art form. The earliest poems were there to commemorate, to remember, across generations, whether a victory in battle, or the life of the tribe. The *Odyssey*, *Beowulf* are poems, yes, but with a practical function. If you can't write it down how will you pass it on? You remember. You recite.

The rhythm and image of poetry make it easier to recall than prose, easier to chant. But I needed prose too, and so I made my own concise versions of nineteenth-century novels – going for the talismanic, not worrying much about the plot.

I had lines inside me – a string of guiding lights. I had language.

Fiction and poetry are doses, medicines. What they heal is the rupture reality makes on the imagination.

I had been damaged and a very important part of me had been destroyed – that was my reality, the facts of my life; but on the other side of the facts was who I could be, how I could feel, and as long as I had words for that, images for that, stories for that, then I wasn't lost.

There was pain. There was joy. There was the painful joy Eliot had written about. My first sense of that painful joy was walking up to the hill above our house, the long stretchy streets with a town at the bottom and a hill at the top. The cobbled streets. The streets that went straight to the Factory Bottoms.

I looked out and it didn't look like a mirror or a world. It was the place I was, not the place where I would be. The books had gone, but they were objects;

what they held could not be so easily destroyed. What they held was already inside me, and together we would get away.

And standing over the smouldering pile of paper and type, still warm the next cold morning, I understood that there was something else I could do.

'Fuck it,' I thought, 'I can write my own.'

5

At Home

OUR HOUSE WAS A NARROW house in a long narrow terrace of houses. The road outside was cobbled. The pavement was laid with solid slabs of York stone. Our house, number 200, was almost at the top.

Inside the house was a tight dark lobby with a line of coat hooks and a coin-slot gas meter. Off the lobby to the right was the best parlour, distinguished by a standard lamp, a radiogram, a vinyl three-piece suite and a display cabinet.

Pass by this door and there were steep stairs leading upwards. Go straight ahead and that was our living room, our kitchen, our yard, our coal-hole, and our outside loo, known as the Betty.

Upstairs were two bedrooms, one to the right and one to the left. When I was fourteen, the damp, leaking room on the left was divided into a small bedroom for me, and a bathroom for all of us. Until then, we had a slop bucket upstairs. Until then we all slept in the same room. In that room was the double bed where my father slept, and where my mother slept if my father wasn't in it, and a single bed against the wall where I slept. I have always been good at sleeping.

Between the beds was a small table holding a light-up globe lamp on my side, and a light-up ballerina electric twirling alarm clock lamp and bedside light on her side.

Mrs Winterson loved multi-purpose electrical goods of hideous design. She was one of the first women to have a heated corset. Unfortunately, when it overheated it beeped to warn the user. As the corset was by definition underneath her petticoat, dress, apron and coat, there was little she could do to cool down except take off her coat and stand in the yard. If it rained she had to stand in the Betty.

It was a good loo; whitewashed and compact with a flashlight hanging behind the door. I smuggled books in here and read them in secret, claiming constipation. That was risky because Mrs W was keen on suppositories and enemas. But there is always a price to pay for your art . . .

The coal-hole was not a good place; leaky, dirty, cold. I hated being locked in there much more than I hated being locked out on the doorstep. I used to shout and bang on the door but this had no effect. I once managed to break the door down, but that was followed by a beating. My mother never beat me. She waited until my father came home and told him how many strokes and what with . . . the plastic cane, the belt, or just his hand.

Sometimes a whole day went by before the punishment was meted out, and so crime and punishment seemed disconnected to me, and the punishment arbitrary and pointless. I didn't respect them for it. I didn't fear it after a while. It did not modify my behaviour. It did make me hate them – not all the time – but with the hatred of the helpless; a flaring, subsiding hatred that gradually became the bed of the relationship.

A hatred made of coal, and burning low like coal, and fanned up every time there was another crime, another punishment.

The working-class north of England was a routinely brutal world. Men hit women – or as D. H. Lawrence called it, gave them 'a dab' – to keep them in their place. Less often, but not unknown, women hit men, and if it was in the general morality of 'I deserved that' – drunkenness, womanising, gambling the house-keeping money – then the men accepted the thump.

Kids were slapped most days but beatings were less common. Kids fought all the time – boys and girls alike – and I grew up not caring much about physical pain. I used to hit my girlfriends until I realised it was not acceptable. Even now, when I am furious, what I would like to do is to punch the infuriating person flat on the ground.

That solves nothing, I know, and I've spent a lot of time understanding my own violence, which is not of the pussycat kind. There are people who could never commit murder. I am not one of those people.

It is better to know it. Better to know who you are, and what lies in you, what you could do, might do, under extreme provocation.

My father started hitting his second wife a few years after they were married. Lillian called me at home in the Cotswolds and said, 'Your dad's started throwing things. I threw some back.'

They were living in a sheltered accommodation bungalow by then, an unlikely scene of domestic violence, and my dad was seventy-seven. I didn't

take it seriously. What were they throwing? False
teeth?

I know that he used to hit my mother before they
found Jesus, and I know that both she and her own
mother were knocked about by my grandad, but when
I was growing up, Dad only hit me when he was
under instruction from my mother.

The next day I made the four-hour trip to Accrington,
and Dad was sent out to buy fish and chips. Lillian
made me a cup of tea and gave it to me in a plastic
cup. There was broken crockery all over the place.

'My tea set,' said Lillian, 'what's left of it . . . and
bought and paid for with my own money, not his.'

She was indignant, especially as Mrs Winterson
had collected Royal Albert china all her life – a very
nasty set of sentimental tableware kept in the display
cabinet. Lillian had persuaded Dad to sell it and start
again.

Lillian had bruises. Dad was looking sheepish.

I took him out in the car to the Trough of Bowland.
He loved the hills and valleys of Lancashire – we both
did. When he was a vigorous man he used to carry
me on the parcel rack of his push bike about ten
miles till we reached Pendle Hill, then we'd walk and
walk all day. Those were my happiest times.

He had never talked much, him being clumsy and
unsure with language, and my mum and me fast-draw
and furious in our arguments and exchanges. But I
suspect it was Mrs Winterson's own Jehovah-like
conversational style – really a lifelong soliloquy – that
had silenced him further than his own nature allowed.

I asked him what had been happening with the
crockery, and he didn't say anything for about half an

hour, then he cried. We had some tea out of the flask, and he started talking about the war.

He had been in the D-Day landings. He was in the first wave of the assault. They had no ammunition, only their bayonets. He killed six men with his bayonet.

He told me about coming home on leave to Liverpool. He had been so tired that he had just walked into an empty abandoned house, pulled down the curtains and covered himself up on the settee. He had been woken at dawn by a policeman shaking his shoulder – did he not know what had happened?

Dad looked all round, still half asleep. He was on the settee under the curtains, but the house had gone. It had been bombed in the night.

He told me about his father walking him round and round the Liverpool docks looking for work in the Depression. Dad was born in 1919, he was a celebratory end-of-First-World-War baby, and then they forgot to celebrate him. They forgot to look after him at all. He was the generation reared in time for the next war.

He was twenty when he was called up. He knew about neglect and poverty, and he knew that you had to hit life before it hit you.

Somehow, all of those parts of Dad that had sunk to the bottom for so many years had come to the top again. And with them had come bad dreams about Mrs Winterson and their early married life.

'I did love her . . .' he kept saying.

'You did, and now you love Lillian, and you mustn't throw the teapot at her.'

'Connie won't forgive me for marrying again.'

'It's all right, Dad. She'll be glad you're happy.'

'No, she won't.'

And I'm thinking, unless heaven is more than a place, unless it's a full personality transplant, no, she won't . . . but I don't say that. Instead we eat chocolate and go quiet. Then he says, 'I've been frightened.'

'Don't be frightened, Dad.'

'No, no,' he nods, comforted, a little boy. He was always a little boy, and I am upset that I didn't look after him, upset that there are so many kids who never get looked after, and so they can't grow up. They can get older, but they can't grow up. That takes love. If you are lucky the love will come later. If you are lucky you won't hit love in the face.

He said he wouldn't do it again. I took Lillian to buy some new crockery.

'I like these beaker . . .' she said. And I like it that she calls mugs 'beakers'. It's a good slang – something to dip your beak in.

'I blame Connie,' she said. 'They should have locked her up for what she did to you and your dad. You know she was mad don't you? All that Jesus and staying up all night and throwing you out of the house and the gun and the corsets and bits of the bloody Bible stuck up everywhere. I made him scrape them off the walls y'know. He always loved you but she wouldn't let him. He never wanted you to go.'

'He didn't fight for me, Lillian.'

'I know, I know, I've told him . . . and that horrible house . . . and that horrible Royal Albert.'

My mother had married down. Marrying down meant no money and no prospects. Marrying down meant showing everyone else in the street that even though you weren't better off, you were better. Being better meant a display cabinet.

Every spare penny went into a biscuit tin marked ROYAL ALBERT, and every bit of Royal Albert went into the display cabinet.

Royal Albert is covered in roses and edged with gold. Needless to say we only used it at Christmas and on my mother's birthday, which was in January. The rest of the time it was *displayed*.

We all caught Royal Albert fever. I saved up. Dad did overtime, and we did it because every presentation of a plate or a gravy boat made her as close to happy as she could ever be. Happiness was still on the other side of a glass door, but at least she could see it through the glass, like a prisoner being visited by a longed-for loved one.

She wanted to be happy, and I think that is a lot of why I enraged her as much as I did. I just couldn't live in the cosmic dustbin with the lid on. While her favourite chorus was 'God Has Blotted Them Out', mine was 'Cheer Up Ye Saints of God'.

I still sing it and I have taught it to all my friends and my godchildren, and it is completely ridiculous and, I think, rather wonderful. Here are all the words:

> Cheer up ye saints of God,
> There's nothing to worry about;
> Nothing to make you feel afraid,
> Nothing to make you doubt;
> Remember Jesus saves you;
> So why not trust him and shout,

You'll be sorry you worried at all, tomorrow morning.

So, there was my mum at the piano singing 'God Has Blotted Them Out', and there was me in the coal-hole singing 'Cheer Up Ye Saints of God'.

The trouble with adoption is that you never know what you are going to get.

Our life at home was a bit odd.

I didn't go to school until I was five, because we were living in Grandad's house and looking after the dying grandmother. School was too difficult to add.

In the days of the dying Grandmother I used to climb on her big high bed in the sitting room that looked onto the rose garden. It was a lovely light room and I was always the first person awake.

In the way that small children and old people can be so well matched, I loved getting into the kitchen and standing on a stool and making really messy jam and cream sandwiches. These were all my grandmother could eat, because of her throat cancer. I liked them, but I liked anything that was food, and besides, at that hour there were none of the Dead hanging round the kitchen. Or maybe it was only my mother who could see them.

When the sandwiches were made I took them to the big high bed – I was about four, I suppose – and woke up Grandma and we ate them and got jam everywhere and read. She read to me and I read to her. I was good at reading – you have to be if you start with the Bible . . . but I loved words from the beginning.

She bought me all the *Orlando the Marmalade Cat* books by Kathleen Hale. He was so very orange and debonair.

Those days were good. One day my father's mother came to visit and was introduced to me as 'your grandmother'.

I said, 'I've got one grandmother, I don't want another one.'

It really hurt her and my dad, and was more proof positive of my evil nature. But no one thought to see that in my small arithmetic two mothers had meant the first one gone forever. Why would two grand-mothers not mean the same?

I was so frightened of loss.

When Grandma died I found her. I didn't know she was dead. I just knew that she wasn't reading the story or eating the jam and cream sandwiches.

And then we packed our bags and left Grandad's house with the three gardens and the steep wood behind.

We moved back to Water Street. The two-up two-down.

My mother's depression started then, I think.

During the sixteen years that I lived at home, my father was on shift work at the factory, or he was at church. That was his pattern.

My mother was awake all night and depressed all day. That was her pattern.

I was at school, at church, out in the hills, or reading in secret. That was my pattern.

I learned secrecy early. To hide my heart. To conceal my thoughts. Once it had been decided that I was the Wrong Crib, everything I did supported my mother in that belief. She watched me for signs of possession.

When I went deaf she didn't take me to the doctor because she knew it was either Jesus stoppering up my ears to the things of the world in an attempt to reform my broken soul, or it was Satan whispering so loud that he had perforated my eardrums.

It was very bad for me that my deafness happened at around the same time as I discovered my clitoris.

Mrs W was nothing if not old-fashioned. She knew that masturbation made you blind, so it was not difficult to conclude that it made you deaf too.

I thought this was unfair as a lot of people we knew had hearing aids and glasses.

In the public library there was an entire large-print section. I noticed it was next to the individual study cubicles. Presumably one thing led to another.

In any event, I did have to have my adenoids out, so it was neither Jesus nor Satan who had blocked my ears, leaving only my own base nature as the culprit.

When my mother took me to the hospital and settled me in the high-sided bed on the children's ward, I climbed straight out and ran after her.

She was up ahead in her Crimplene coat, tall, massy, solitary, and I can still feel the polished lino skidding under my bare feet.

Panic. I can feel it now. I must have thought she had taken me back to be adopted again.

I remember that afternoon in hospital and being given the anaesthetic and starting to make up a story about a rabbit that had no fur. His mother gave him a jewelled coat to wear but a weasel stole it and it was winter . . .

I suppose I should finish that story one day . . .

It took me a long time to realise that there are two kinds of writing: the one you write and the one that writes you. The one that writes you is dangerous. You go where you don't want to go. You look where you don't want to look.

After the rabbit and adenoids episode I was sent to school a year late. This was a worry because my mother called it the Breeding Ground – and when I asked her what exactly a Breeding Ground was, she said it was like the sink would be if she didn't put bleach down it.

She told me not to mix with the other children, who presumably had survived the bleach – anyway they were all very pale.

I could read and write and add up and that was all that happened at school. In spite of my competence I was given bad reports in the way that bad children are given bad reports. I had accepted the *bad* label. It was better to have some identity than none at all.

Most of the time I drew pictures of Hell which I took home for my mother to admire. There is a very nice technique for Hell: colour a piece of paper with lots of bright rainbow colours in blocks then get a black wax crayon and scrub out all the colours. Then get a pin and etch into the paper. Where the black is scraped away the colours come through. Dramatic and effective. Especially for lost souls.

★

When I left the infant school in disgrace for burning down the play kitchen, the headmistress, who wore black tweed because she was in mourning for Scotland, told my mother that I was domineering and aggressive.

I was. I beat up the other kids, boys and girls alike, and when I couldn't understand what was being said to me in a lesson I just left the classroom and bit the teachers if they tried to make me come back.

I realise my behaviour wasn't ideal but my mother believed I was demon possessed and the headmistress was in mourning for Scotland. It was hard to be normal.

I got myself up for school every day. My mother left me a bowl of cornflakes and the milk in a flask. We had no fridge and most of the year we had no need of one – the house was cold, the North was cold, and when we bought food we ate it.

Mrs Winterson had terrible stories about fridges – they gave off gas and made you dizzy, mice got caught in the motor, rats would be attracted by the dead mice caught in the motor . . . children got trapped inside and couldn't escape – she knew of a family whose youngest child had climbed into the fridge to play hide-and-seek, and frozen to death. They had to defrost the fridge to prise him out. After that the council took away the other children. I wondered why they didn't just take away the fridge.

Every morning when I came downstairs I blew on the fire to get it going and read my note – there was always a note. The note began with a general reminder about washing – HANDS, FACE, NECK AND

EARS – and an exhortation from the Bible, such as *Seek Ye the Lord*. Or *Watch and Pray*.

The exhortation was different every day. The body parts to be washed stayed the same.

When I was seven we got a dog, and my job before school was to walk the dog round the block and feed her. So then the list was arranged as WASH, WALK, FEED, READ.

At dinner time, as lunchtime was called in the North, I came home from school for the first few years, because junior school was only round the corner. By then, my mother was up and about, and we ate pie and peas and had a Bible reading.

Later, when I was at the grammar school further away, I didn't come home at dinner time, and so I didn't have any dinner. My mother refused to be means-tested, and so I didn't qualify for free school meals, but we had no money to buy the meals either. I usually took a couple of slices of white bread and a bit of cheese, just like that, in my bag.

Nobody thought it unusual – and it wasn't. There were plenty of kids who didn't get fed properly.

We did get fed properly in the evening because we had an allotment, and our vegetables were good. I liked growing vegetables – I still do, and there is a quiet pleasure in it for me. We had hens, so got eggs, but with meat affordable only twice a week, we didn't get enough protein.

Thursday nights were always boiled onions or boiled potatoes from the allotment. Dad got paid Fridays and by Thursday there was no money left. In winter, the gas and electricity meters ran out on Thursdays too, and so the onions and potatoes weren't quite boiled enough and we ate them in the dark of the paraffin lamp.

Everybody in the street was the same. Blackout Thursdays were common.

We had no car, no phone, and no central heating. In winter the windows froze on the inside.

We were usually cold but I don't remember being upset by it. My dad had had no socks when he was a little boy, so our feet, if not the rest of us, had made progress.

We had a coal fire that I learned to lay and to light when I was five, as soon as we moved back from Grandad's centrally heated house to our own draughty and damp terrace. My dad taught me how to make a fire and I was so proud of myself and my burnt fingers and singed hair.

It was my job to make twists of paper and soak them in paraffin and keep them stacked in a sealed biscuit tin. Dad collected kindling and axed it up. When the coalman came he gave my mother free bags of the stuff they called slack because he had wanted to marry her. She viewed this as an insult to her moral character but she kept the slack.

When my mother went to bed – around six in the morning – she spread the thin dusty tarry slack over the fire to keep it low and hot, and left coal for me to get the fire going again at 7.30 a.m. She sat up all night listening to secret broadcasts of the Gospel to Soviet Russia behind the Iron Curtain. She baked, she sewed, she knitted, she mended, and she read the Bible.

She was such a solitary woman. A solitary woman

who longed for one person to know her. I think I do know her now, but it is too late.

Or is it?

Freud, one of the grand masters of narrative, knew that the past is not fixed in the way that linear time suggests. We can return. We can pick up what we dropped. We can mend what others broke. We can talk with the dead.

Mrs Winterson left behind things that she could not do.

One of those things was to make a home.

The Romanian philosopher Mircea Eliade talks about home – ontological as well as geographical home – and in a lovely phrase, he calls home 'the heart of the real'.

Home, he tells us, is the intersection of two lines – the vertical and the horizontal. The vertical plane has heaven, or the upper world, at one end, and the world of the dead at the other end. The horizontal plane is the traffic of this world, moving to and fro – our own traffic and that of teeming others.

Home was a place of order. A place where the order of things come together – the living and dead – the spirits of the ancestors and the present inhabitants, and the gathering up and stilling of all the to-and-fro.

Leaving home can only happen because there is a home to leave. And the leaving is never just a geograph-ical or spatial separation; it is an emotional separation – wanted or unwanted. Steady or ambivalent.

For the refugee, for the homeless, the lack of this crucial coordinate in the placing of the self has severe consequences. At best it must be managed, made up for in some way. At worst, a displaced person, literally, does not know which way is up, because there is no true north. No compass point. Home is much more than shelter; home is our centre of gravity.

A nomadic people learn to take their homes with them – and the familiar objects are spread out or re-erected from place to place. When we move house, we take with us the invisible concept of home – but it is a very powerful concept. Mental health and emotional continuity do not require us to stay in the same house or the same place, but they do require a sturdy structure on the inside – and that structure is built in part by what has happened on the outside. The inside and the outside of our lives are each the shell where we learn to live.

Home was problematic for me. It did not represent order and it did not stand for safety. I left home at sixteen, and after that I was always moving, until finally, almost by accident, I found and kept two places, both modest, one in London and one in the country. I have never lived with anyone in either of those homes.

I am not entirely happy about that, but when I did live with someone, and for thirteen years, I could only manage it by having a lot of separate space. I am not messy, I am organised, and I cook and clean very happily, but another presence is hard for me. I wish it were not so, because I would really like to live with someone I love.

I just don't think I know how to do that.

So it is better to accept my not quite adjusted need for distance and privacy.

Mrs Winterson never respected my privacy. She

ransacked my possessions, read my diaries, my note-books, my stories, my letters. I never felt safe in the house and when she made me leave it I felt betrayed. The horrible sick feeling that I had never belonged and never would belong is assuaged now by the fact that my homes are mine and I can come and go as I please.

I never had a key to the house in Water Street, and so entry depended on being let in – or not. I don't know why I am still so fond of doorsteps – it seems perverse, given that I spent so much time sitting on one, but the two parts of home that mattered to me in Accrington are the parts I could least do without now.

They are the threshold and the hearth.

My friends joke that I won't shut the door unless it is officially bedtime or actually snowing into the kitchen. The first thing I do when I get up in the morning is to open the back door. The next thing I do, in winter, is to light the fire.

All those hours spent sitting on my bum on the doorstep have given me a feeling for liminal space. I love the way cats like to be half in half out, the wild and the tame, and I too am the wild and the tame. I am domestic, but only if the door is open.

And I guess that is the key – no one is ever going to lock me in or lock me out again. My door is open and I am the one who opens it.

The threshold and the hearth are mythic spaces. Each has sacred and ceremonial aspects in the history of our myth. To cross the threshold is to enter another world – whether the one on the inside or the one on the outside – and we can never be really sure what is on the other side of the door until we open it.

Everyone has dreams of familiar doors and unknown rooms. Narnia is through a door in a wardrobe. In the story of Bluebeard there is one door that must not be opened. A vampire cannot cross a threshold strewn with garlic. Open the door into the tiny Tardis, and inside is a vast and changing space.

The tradition of carrying the bride into her new house is a rite of passage; one world has been left behind, another entered. When we leave the parental home, even now, we do much more than go out of the house with a suitcase.

Our own front door can be a wonderful thing, or a sight we dread; rarely is it only a door.

The crossing in and out, the different worlds, the significant spaces, are private coordinates that in my fiction I have tried to make paradigmatic.

Personal stories work for other people when those stories become both paradigms and parables. The intensity of a story – say the story in *Oranges* – releases into a bigger space than the one it occupied in time and place. The story crosses the threshold from my world into yours. We meet each other on the steps of the story.

Books, for me, are a home. Books don't make a home – they are one, in the sense that just as you do with a door, you open a book, and you go inside. Inside there is a different kind of time and a different kind of space.

There is warmth there too – a hearth. I sit down with a book and I am warm. I know that from the chilly nights on the doorstep.

Mrs Winterson lived in the same house on Water Street from 1947 until her death in 1990. Was it a sanctuary? I don't think so. Was it where she wanted to be? No . . .

She hated the small and the mean, and yet that is all she had. I bought a few big houses myself along the way, simply because I was trying out something for her. In fact, my tastes are more modest – but you don't know that until you have bought and sold for the ghost of your mother.

Like most people I lived for a long time with my mother and father . . . that's how *Oranges* begins, and it ends with the young woman, let's call her Jeanette, returning home to find things much the same – a new electronic organ to add a bit of bass and percussion to the Christmas carols, but otherwise, it's life as it ever was – the giant figure of the mother stooped inside the cramped house, filling it with Royal Albert and electrical goods, totting up the church accounts in a double ledger, smoking into the night underneath a haze of fly spray, her fags hidden in a box marked RUBBER BANDS.

Like most people, when I look back, the family house is held in time, or rather it is now outside of time, because it exists so clearly and it does not change, and it can only be entered through a door in the mind.

I like it that pre-industrial societies, and religious cultures still, now, distinguish between two kinds of time – linear time, that is also cyclical because history repeats itself, even as it seems to progress, and real time, which is not subject to the clock or the calendar, and is where the soul used to live. This real time is reversible and redeemable. It is why, in religious rites of all kinds, something that happened once is re-enacted – Passover, Christmas, Easter, or, in the pagan record, Midsummer and the dying of the god. As we participate in the ritual, we step outside of linear time and enter real time.

Time is only truly locked when we live in a mechanised world. Then we turn into clock-watchers and time-servers. Like the rest of life, time becomes uniform and standardised.

When I left home at sixteen I bought a small rug. It was my roll-up world. Whatever room, whatever temporary place I had, I unrolled the rug. It was a map of myself. Invisible to others, but held in the rug, were all the places I had stayed – for a few weeks, for a few months. On the first night anywhere new I liked to lie in bed and look at the rug to remind myself that I had what I needed even though what I had was so little.

Sometimes you have to live in precarious and temporary places. Unsuitable places. Wrong places. Sometimes the safe place won't help you.

Why did I leave home when I was sixteen? It was one of those important choices that will change the rest of your life. When I look back it feels like I was at the borders of common sense, and the sensible thing to do would have been to keep quiet, keep going, learn to lie better and leave later.

I have noticed that doing the sensible thing is only a good idea when the decision is quite small. For the life-changing things, you must risk it.

And here is the shock – when you risk it, when you do the right thing, when you arrive at the borders of common sense and cross into unknown territory, leaving behind you all the familiar smells and lights, then you do not experience great joy and huge energy.

You are unhappy. Things get worse.

It is a time of mourning. Loss. Fear. We bullet ourselves through with questions. And then we feel shot and wounded.

And then all the cowards come out and say, 'See, I told you so.'

In fact, they told you nothing.

6

Church

'THAT'S NOT A CHURCH — THAT'S two terraced houses knocked together.'

Elim Pentecostal Church, Blackburn Road, Accrington, was the centre of my life for sixteen years. It had no pews, no altar, no nave or chancel, no stained glass, no candles, no organ.

It had fold-up wooden chairs, a long low pulpit — more like a stage than the traditional box on stilts — a pub piano and a pit.

The pit could be filled with water for our baptismal services. Just as Jesus had baptised his disciples in the River Jordan, we too fully immersed believers in a deep warm plunge pool which had to be slowly heated up the day before the service.

Baptismal candidates were given a little box for their teeth and spectacles. It had been spectacles only until Mrs Smalley opened her mouth underwater to praise the Lord and lost her top teeth. The pastor couldn't swim so a member of the flock had to dive down and pull them out — we all sang 'I Will Make You Fishers of Men' as an encouragement, but it was felt that while losing one set of teeth was a misfortune, to lose two sets looked liked carelessness. And so baptism happened without dentures — if you had them, and most people had them.

There was a fierce debate about burial/cremation with or without the dentures.

Like most evangelical groups, Elim believed in the resurrection of the body at the Last Trump – Mrs Winterson did not, but kept quiet. The question was, if you had had your teeth removed, and that was a fashionable thing to do until the 1960s, would you get them back at the Last Trump? If you did, would the falsies be in the way? If not, would you have to spend eternity with no teeth?

Some said it didn't matter because nobody would be eating in the afterlife; others said it mattered a lot because we would want to look our best for Jesus . . .

And on it went . . .

Mrs Winterson didn't want her body resurrected because she had never, ever loved it, not even for a single minute of a single day. But although she believed in End Time, she felt that the bodily resurrection was unscientific. When I asked her about this she told me she had seen Pathé newsreels of Hiroshima and Nagasaki, and she knew all about Robert Oppenheimer and the Manhattan Project. She had lived through the war. Her brother had been in the air force, my dad had been in the army – it was their life, not their history. She said that after the atomic bomb you couldn't believe in mass any more, it was all about energy. 'This life is all mass. When we go, we'll be all energy, that's all there is to it.'

I have thought about this a lot over the years. She had understood something infinitely complex and absolutely simple. For her, in the Book of Revelation, the 'things of the world' that would pass away, 'heaven and earth rolled up like a scroll', were demonstrations of the inevitable movement from mass to energy. Her uncle, her beloved mother's beloved brother, had been a scientist. She was an intelligent woman, and some-where in the middle of the insane theology and the brutal politics, the flamboyant depression and the refusal of books, of knowledge, of life, she had watched the atomic bomb go off and realised that the true nature of the world is energy not mass.

But she never understood that energy could have been her own true nature while she was alive. She did not need to be trapped in mass.

Baptismal candidates wore a white sheet, either sheep-ishly or rakishly, and were asked this simple question by the pastor: 'Do you accept the Lord Jesus Christ as your saviour?'

The answer was: 'I do.' At this point the candidate waded into the water and, while held on either side by two strong men, was fully submerged – dying to the old life, surfacing into the new day. Once upright again and soaked through, they were given back their teeth and glasses and sent to dry off in the kitchen.

Baptismal services were very popular and were always followed by a supper of potato pie and mincemeat.

The Elim Church does not baptise infants. Baptism is for adults, or those somewhere near adulthood – I was thirteen. No one can be baptised by Elim unless they have given their lives to Jesus and understand what that means. Christ's injunction that his followers must be twice-born, the natural birth and the spiritual birth, is in keeping with religious initiation ceremonies both pagan and tribal. There has to be a rite of passage, and a conscious one, between the life given by chance and circumstance and the life that is chosen.

There are psychological advantages to choosing life and a way of life consciously – and not just accepting life as an animal gift lived according to the haphazard of nature and chance. The 'second birth' protects the psyche by prompting both self-reflection and meaning.

I know that the whole process very easily becomes another kind of rote learning, where nothing is chosen at all, and any answers, however daft, are preferred to honest questioning. But the principle remains good. I saw a lot of working-class men and women – myself included – living a deeper, more thoughtful life than would have been possible without the Church. These were not educated people; Bible study worked their brains. They met after work in noisy discussion. The sense of belonging to something big, something important, lent unity and meaning.

A meaningless life for a human being has none of the dignity of animal unselfconsciousness; we cannot simply eat, sleep, hunt and reproduce – we are meaning-seeking creatures. The Western world has done away with religion but not with our religious impulses; we seem to need some higher purpose, some point to our lives – money and leisure, social progress, are just not enough.

We shall have to find new ways of finding meaning – it is not yet clear how this will happen.

But for the members of the Elim Pentecostal Church in Accrington, life was full of miracles, signs, wonders, and practical purpose.

That was how the movement had started in 1915,

in Monaghan, Ireland, though the founder, George Jeffreys, was a Welshman. The name Elim comes from Exodus 15:27. Moses is trudging through the desert with the Israelites and everyone is miserable, tired and looking for a sign from God, when suddenly, *they came to Elim, where were twelve wells of water and threescore and ten palm trees: and they encamped there by the waters.*

If a hen wasn't laying – pray over her and an egg was sure to follow. Our Easter services always blessed the hens, and a lot of people kept them; ours were in our allotment, most were in people's backyards. A visitation by a fox soon turned into a parable about the sneak-thief ways of Satan. A hen that wouldn't lay however often you prayed over her was like a soul who turned from Jesus – proud and unproductive.

If you pegged out your washing and it rained – get a few of the faithful to pray for a good drying wind. As nobody had a telephone we often turned up at each other's houses asking for help. Not Mrs Winterson – she prayed alone, and she prayed standing up, more like an Old Testament prophet than a sinner on her knees.

Her suffering was her armour. Gradually it became her skin. Then she could not take it off. She died without painkillers and in pain.

For the rest of us, for me, the certainty of a nearby God made sense of the uncertainty. We had no bank accounts, no phones, no cars, no inside toilets, often no carpets, no job security and very little money. The church was a place of mutual help and imaginative possibility. I don't know anyone, including me, who felt trapped or hopeless. What did it matter if we had one pair of shoes and no food on Thursday nights before payday? *Seek ye first the kingdom of God and all these things shall be added unto you* . . .

Good advice – if the kingdom of God is the place of true value, the place not bound by the facts and figures of the everyday, if it is what you love for its own sake . . .

In a world that has become instrumental and utilitarian, the symbol of the kingdom of God – and it is a symbol not a place – stands as the challenge of love to the arrogance of power and the delusions of wealth.

Monday night – Sisterhood
Tuesday night – Bible Study
Wednesday night – Prayer Meeting
Thursday night – Brotherhood/Black and
   Decker
Friday night – Youth Group
Saturday night – Revival Meeting (away)
Sunday – All day

The Brothers' Black and Decker nights were practical meetings to fix up the church building or to help one of the brothers at home. The Saturday-night revival meetings were really the highlight of the week because that usually meant a trip to another church, or, in the summer, a tent crusade.

Our church had a giant tent and every summer we went up and down with the Glory Crusade. My mother and father had remade their marriage in a Glory Crusade tent on a piece of spare land under the Accrington viaduct.

My mother loved the Glory Crusades. I don't think

she believed half of what she was supposed to believe, and she made up quite a lot of theology. But I think that the night in the tent crusade when she and Dad found the Lord stopped her walking away from home with a small suitcase and never coming back.

And so every year when Mrs Winterson saw the tent in the field, and heard the harmonium playing 'Abide With Me', she used to grab my hand and say, 'I can smell Jesus.'

The smell of the canvas (it always rains up north in the summer), and the smell of soup cooking for afterwards, and the smell of damp paper printed with the hymns – that's what Jesus smells like.

If you want to save souls – and who doesn't – then a tent seems to be the best kind of temporary structure. It is a metaphor for this provisional life of ours – without foundations and likely to blow over. It is a romance with the elements. The wind blows, the tent billows, who here feels lost and alone? Answer – all of us. The harmonium plays 'What A Friend We Have in Jesus'.

In a tent you feel a sympathy with the others even when you don't know them. The fact of being in a tent together is a kind of bond, and when you see smiling faces and when you smell the soup, and the person next to you asks your name, then quite likely you will want to be saved. The smell of Jesus is a good one.

The tent was like the war had been for all the people of my parents' age. Not real life, but a time where ordinary rules didn't apply. You could forget the bills and the bother. You had a common purpose.

I can see them; Dad in his knitted cardigan and knitted tie standing at the flap shaking hands with people as they came in; Mother, halfway up the tent aisle, helping people to find a seat.

And there's me, giving out hymn sheets or leading the choruses – evangelical churches sing a lot of choruses – short sharp merry verses with rousing tunes – easy to memorise. Like 'Cheer Up Ye Saints of God'.

It is hard to understand the contradictions unless you have lived them; the camaraderie, the simple happiness, the kindness, the sharing, the pleasure of something to do every night in a town where there was nothing to do – then set this against the cruelty of dogma, the miserable rigidity of no drink, no fags, no sex (or if you were married, as little sex as possible), no going to the pictures (an exception was made for Charlton Heston as Moses in *The Ten Commandments*), no reading anything except devotional literature, no fancy clothes (not that we could afford them), no dancing (unless it was in church, and it was a kind of Irish jig of godly ecstasy), no pop music, no card games, no pubs – even for orange juice. TV was OK but not on Sundays. On Sundays you covered the set with a cloth.

But I loved it in the school holidays when the Glory Crusades were on and you could get on your bike and cycle thirty or forty miles to wherever the tent was and somebody would give you a sausage or a pie, and then it was time for the meeting, and hours later everybody who had travelled got in their sleeping bags and went to sleep on the floor. Then we biked home again.

Mrs Winterson came by coach on her own so that she could smoke.

One day she brought Auntie Nellie with her. They both smoked but they had a pact not to tell anybody. Auntie Nellie had been a Methodist but she had changed her mind. Everybody called her Auntie Nellie even though she had no biological family. I think she was born called Auntie Nellie.

She lived in a slum tenement of one-up one-down stone-built factory dwellings. The outside loo was shared with two other houses. It was very clean – outside loos were supposed to be very clean – and this one had a picture of the young Queen Elizabeth II in military uniform. Someone had graffitied GOD BLESS HER on the wall.

Auntie Nellie shared the loo but she had her own outside tap that gave her cold water and inside there was a coal-burning iron range with a great big tin kettle on it, and a heavy flat iron. We supposed she still used the flat iron to press her clothes, and at night she put the flat iron in her bed to warm it up.

She was unmarried, bow-legged, frizzy-haired, thin like someone who never has quite enough to eat, and she was never seen without her coat on.

When the women came to lay her out they had to cut the buttons on her coat to get it off and they said it was more like corrugated iron than tweed.

Then we found out that she wore woollen underwear, including a liberty bodice, woollen stockings, and a kind of patchwork petticoat made of bits and pieces – I think she sewed bits on and cut bits off over the years. There was a thick gent's silk scarf round her neck, invisible under her coat, and that was quite a luxury that scarf and led to speculation – had she had a fancy man?

If she had it must have been in the war. Her friend said every woman had had a fancy man in the war – married or not, that's how it was.

However it was, or had been, now she was wearing the scarf and the underwear and the coat and nothing else. No dress, no skirt, no blouse.

We wondered if she had been too ill lately to get dressed, even though she had still been walking up and down to church and to the market. Nobody knew her age.

It was the first time any of us had been upstairs.

The small room was bare – a tiny window with newspaper tacked over it for warmth. A peg-rug on the floorboards – you make those yourself out of scraps of cotton and they have a rough-coated feel and they lie there like downcast dogs.

There was an iron bedstead heaped with lumpy eiderdowns – the kind that were only ever stuffed with one duck.

There was a chair with a dusty hat on it. There was a slop bucket for the night. There was a photograph on the wall of Auntie Nellie as a young woman wearing a black-and-white polka-dot dress.

There was a cupboard and in the cupboard were two clean sets of darned underclothes and two clean pairs of thick woollen stockings. Hanging up and wrapped in brown paper was the polka-dot dress. It had sweat pads sewn into the armpits the way they used to do before deodorant. You just washed out the pads along with your stockings at night.

We looked and we looked but there wasn't anywhere to look. Auntie Nellie had kept her coat on because she had no clothes.

The women washed her and they put her in the polka-dot dress. They showed me how to make a body look nice. It wasn't my first body – I had sat eating jam sandwiches with Dead Grandma, and in the North in the 1960s coffins were kept open at home for three days and nobody minded.

But touching a dead body is odd – I still find it odd – the skin changes so quickly and everything shrinks. Yet I would not give up the body I love to a stranger to wash and dress. It is the last thing you can do for someone, and the last thing you can do together – both your bodies, as it used to be. No, it's not for a stranger . . .

Auntie Nellie cannot have had much money. Twice a week she had all the neighbourhood children she could squeeze into her one room and she made onion soup or potato soup and all the children brought their own cup and she ladled it out off the stove.

She taught them songs and she told them Bible stories and thirty or forty skinny hungry kids queued outside and sometimes brought things from their mothers – buns or toffees – and everybody shared. They all had nits. They all loved her and she loved them. She called her dank dark little house with its one window and black walls 'Sunshine Corner'.

It was my first lesson in love.

I needed lessons in love. I still do because nothing could be simpler, nothing could be harder, than love.

Unconditional love is what a child should expect from a parent even though it rarely works out that way. I didn't have that, and I was a very nervous watchful child. I was a little thug too because nobody was going to beat me up or see me cry. I couldn't relax at home, couldn't disappear into a humming space where I could be alone in the presence of the other. What with the Departed Dead wandering round the kitchen, and mice masquerading as ectoplasm, and the sudden fits of piano playing, and the sometime-revolver, and the relentless brooding mountain range of my mother, and the scary bedtimes – if Dad was on nights and she came to bed it meant all night with the light on reading about the End Time – and the Apocalypse itself never far away, well, home wasn't really a place where you could relax.

Most kids grow up leaving something out for Santa at Christmas time when he comes down the chimney. I used to make presents for the Four Horsemen of the Apocalypse.

'Will it be tonight, Mum?'

'Ask not for whom the bell tolls.'

Mrs Winterson did not have a soothing personality. Ask for reassurance and it would never come. I never asked her if she loved me. She loved me on those days when she was able to love. I really believe that is the best she could do.

When love is unreliable and you are a child, you assume that it is the nature of love – its quality – to be unreliable. Children do not find fault with their parents until later. In the beginning the love you get is the love that sets.

76

I did not know that love could have continuity. I did not know that human love could be depended upon. Mrs Winterson's god was the God of the Old Testament and it may be that modelling yourself on a deity who demands absolute love from his 'children' but thinks nothing of drowning them (Noah's Ark), attempting to kill the ones who madden him (Moses), and letting Satan ruin the life of the most blameless of them all (Job), is bad for love.

True, God reforms himself and improves thanks to his relationship with human beings, but Mrs Winterson was not an interactive type; she didn't like human beings and she never did reform or improve. She was always striking me down, and then making a cake to put things right, and very often after a lockout we'd walk down to the fish and chip shop the next night and sit on the bench outside eating from the newspaper and watching people come and go.

For most of my life I have behaved in much the same way because that is what I learned about love.

Add to that my own wildness and intensity and love becomes pretty dangerous. I never did drugs, I did love – the crazy reckless kind, more damage than healing, more heartbreak than health. And I fought and hit out and tried to put it right the next day. And I went away without a word and didn't care.

Love is vivid. I never wanted the pale version. Love is full strength. I never wanted the diluted version. I never shied away from love's hugeness but I had no idea that love could be as reliable as the sun. The daily rising of love.

★

Auntie Nellie made love into soup. She didn't want thanks and she wasn't 'doing good'. She fed love on Tuesdays and Thursdays to all the children she could find, and even if the Four Horsemen of the Apocalypse had knocked down the outside loo and ridden into the stone-floored kitchen, they would have been given soup.

I went down to her tiny house sometimes but I never thought about what she was doing. Only later, much later, trying to relearn love, did I start to think about that simple continuity and what it meant. Maybe if I had had children I would have got there faster, but maybe I would have hurt my own kids the way I was hurt.

It is never too late to learn to love.

But it is frightening.

At church we heard about love every day, and one day, after the prayer meeting, an older girl kissed me. It was my first moment of recognition and desire. I was fifteen.

I fell in love – what else is there to do?

We were like any pair of kids of the Romeo and Juliet age and kind – mooning about, meeting secretly, passing notes at school, talking about how we would run away and open a bookshop. We started sleeping together at her house, because her mother worked nights. Then one night she came to stay with me in Water Street, which was very unusual as Mrs Winterson hated visitors.

But Helen came to stay and during the night we got into the same bed. We fell asleep. My mother came in with her flashlight. I remember waking up with the flashlight on our faces, the flashlight like a car headlamp passing across Helen's face to my face. The flashlight playing down the narrow bed and out of the window like a signal.

It *was* a signal. It was the signal at the end of the world.

Mrs Winterson was an eschatologist. She believed in End Time, and she rehearsed it. Our emotional states at home were always close to the edge. Things were usually final. Things were often over. When she caught me stealing money she said, 'I will never trust you again.' She didn't. When she knew I was keeping a diary she said, 'I never had secrets from my mother . . . but I am not your mother, am I?' And after that she never was. When I wanted to learn to play her piano she said, 'When you come back from school I will have sold it.' She had.

But lying in bed, pretending not to see the flashlight, pretending to be asleep, and then burying myself back down into Helen's smell, I could believe that nothing had happened – because in truth it hadn't. Not then.

I didn't know that she had let Helen stay because she was looking for proof. She had intercepted a letter. She had seen us holding hands. She had seen the way we looked at each other. Her mind was corrupt and there was no room in there for the clean free place we had made.

She said nothing the next morning, nor for some time to come. She hardly spoke to me, but she often disappeared into herself. Things were calm, like before an air raid.

And then the air raid happened.

★

It was an ordinary Sunday-morning service. I was a bit late. I noticed everyone was looking at me. We sang, we prayed, and then the pastor said that two of the flock were guilty of abominable sin. He read the passage in Romans 1:26: *The women did change their natural use into that which is against nature* . . .

As soon as he began I knew what was going to happen. Helen burst into tears and ran out of the church. I was told to go with the pastor. He was patient. He was young. I don't think he wanted trouble. But Mrs Winterson wanted trouble and she had enough of the old guard behind her. There was going to be an exorcism.

Nobody could believe that anyone as faithful as I was could have had sex – and with another woman – unless there was a demon involved.

I said there was no demon. I said I loved Helen.

My defiance made things worse. I didn't even know I had a demon whereas Helen spotted hers at once and said yes yes yes. I hated her for that. Was love worth so little that it could be given up so easily?

The answer was yes. The mistake they made at church was to forget that I began my small life ready to be given up. Love didn't hold when I was born, and it was tearing now. I did not want to believe that love was such flimsy stuff. I held on tighter because Helen let go.

Dad wouldn't have anything to do with the exorcism but he didn't try and stop it. He took overtime at the factory and it was my mother who let in the elders for the service of prayer and renunciation. They were doing the praying – I was doing the renouncing. They did their bit. I didn't do mine.

The demon is supposed to pop out and maybe set the curtains on fire or fly into the dog who will foam at the mouth and have to be strangled. On occasions we have known demons inhabit pieces of furniture. There was a radiogram that had a demon in it – every time the poor woman tuned in to *Songs of Praise*, all she could hear were manic cackles. The valves were sent away to be blessed and when they were refitted the demon had gone. It might have been something to do with the soldering but nobody mentioned that.

Demons rot foodstuffs, lurk in mirrors, live in groups where there are any Dens of Vice – public houses and betting shops – and they like butchers' shops. It's the blood . . .

When I was locked in the parlour with the curtains closed and no food or heat for three days I was pretty sure I had no demon. After three days of being prayed over in shifts and not allowed to sleep for more than a few hours at a time, I was beginning to believe that I had all Hell in my heart.

At the end of this ordeal, because I was still stubborn, I was beaten repeatedly by one of the elders. Didn't I understand that I was perverting God's plan for normal sexual relationships?

I said, my mother won't sleep in the same bed as my father – is that a normal sexual relationship?

He shoved me onto my knees to repent those words and I felt the bulge in his suit trousers. He tried to kiss me. He said it would be better than with a girl. A lot better. He put his tongue in my mouth. I bit it. Blood. A lot of blood. Blackout.

I woke up in my own bed in the little room my

mother had made for me when she got a grant to put in a bathroom. I loved my little bedroom but it was not a safe place. My mind felt clean and clear. That was probably the sharpness of hunger but I was sure of what to do. I would do whatever they wanted but only on the outside. On the inside I would build another self – one that they couldn't see. Just like after the burning of the books.

I got up. There was food. I ate it. My mother gave me aspirin.

I said I was sorry. She said, 'What's bred in the bone comes out in the marrow.'

'You mean my mother?'

'She was going with men at sixteen.'

'How do you know that?'

She didn't answer. She said, 'You're not leaving this house by day or night until you promise not to see that girl again.'

I said, 'I promise not to see that girl again.'

That night I went round to Helen's house. It was in darkness. I knocked on the door. No one answered. I waited and waited and after a while she came out from round the back. She was leaning on the white-washed wall. She wouldn't look at me.

Did they hurt you? she said.

Yes. Did they hurt you?

No . . . I told them everything . . . What we did . . .

That was ours not theirs.

I had to tell them.

Kiss me.

I can't.

Kiss me.
Don't come again. Please don't come again.

I walked home the long way round so that I shouldn't
be seen by anyone, by chance, coming from Helen's
house. The chip shop was open and I had enough
money. I bought a bag of chips and sat on a wall.

So this is it – not Heathcliff, not Cathy, not Romeo
and Juliet, not love laid end to end like a road across
the world. I thought we could go anywhere. I thought
we could be map and globe, route and compass. I
thought we were each other's world. I thought . . .

We were not lovers, we were love.

I said that to Mrs Winterson – not then, later. She
understood. It was a terrible thing to say to her. That
is why I said it.

But that night there was only Accrington and the
street lamps and the chips and the buses and the slow
way home. The Accrington buses were painted red
and blue and gold – the colours of the East Lancashire
Regiment – the Accrington Pals, famous for being
tiny and plucky and doomed – they were mowed
down at the Battle of the Somme. The buses still had
their mudguards painted black as a mark of respect.

We have to remember. We mustn't forget.

Will you write to me?

*I don't know you. I can't know you. Please don't come
back.*

I don't know what happened to Helen. She went
away to study theology and married an ex-army man

who was training to be a missionary. I met them once, later. She was smug and neurotic. He was sadistic and unattractive. But I would say that, wouldn't I?

After the exorcism I went into a kind of mute state of misery. I used to take my tent and sleep up by the allotment. I didn't want to be near them. My father was unhappy. My mother was disordered. We were like refugees in our own life.

7

Accrington

ILIVED ON A LONG stretchy street with a town at the bottom and a hill at the top.

The town lies at the foot of Hameldon Hill to the east and the Haslingden hills to the south, and from these hills three brooks descend westward, north-west and north to join near the old church, and as one stream flow west to the Hyndburn. The town grew up along the road from Clitheroe to Haslingden and the south, here called Whalley Road, Abbey Street and Manchester Road in succession.

from *A History of the County of Lancaster: Volume 6*, by William Farrer & J. Brownbill (eds), 1911

The first mention of Accrington is in the Domesday Book, and it seems to be an oak-enclosed space. The soil is the heavy clay that oaks enjoy. The land was rough pasture – sheep not arable – but like the rest of Lancashire, Accrington made its money out of cotton.

James Hargreaves, the Lancashire illiterate who invented the spinning jenny in 1764, was baptised and married in Accrington, though he came from

Oswaldtwistle (pronounced Ozzle-twizzle). The spinning jenny was able to do the work of eight spinning wheels, and is really the start of the Lancashire looms and Lancashire's grip on the world cotton trade.

Oswaldtwistle was the next settlement along the road from Accrington and supposedly a place for imbeciles and morons. We called it Gobbin-Land. When I was growing up there was a dog-biscuit factory there, and the poor kids used to hang about outside waiting for sacks of oddments to eat. If you spit on a dog biscuit and dip it in icing sugar it tastes like a proper biscuit.

At our girls' grammar school we were constantly threatened with a future at the dog-biscuit factory in Gobbin-Land. This did not stop the poorer girls bringing dog biscuits to school. The problem was the telltale bone shape, and for a while the school had a policy of No Dog Biscuits.

My mother was a snob and she didn't like me mixing with dog-biscuit girls from Oswaldtwistle. Truthfully, she didn't like me mixing with anyone, and always said, 'We are called to be apart.' That seemed to mean apart from everyone and everything, unless it was the Church. In a small northern town where everybody knows everybody's business, being apart is a full-time job. But my mother needed an occupation.

We went past Woolworths – 'A Den of Vice.' Past Marks and Spencer's – 'The Jews killed Christ.' Past the funeral parlour and the pie shop – 'They share an oven.' Past the biscuit stall and its moon-faced owners – 'Incest.' Past the pet parlour – 'Bestiality.' Past the bank – 'Usury.' Past the Citizens Advice Bureau

– 'Communists.' Past the day nursery – 'Unmarried mothers.' Past the hairdresser's – 'Vanity.' Past the pawn-broker's where my mother had once tried to pawn her leftover solid gold tooth, and on at last to a caff called the Palatine for beans on toast.

My mother loved eating beans on toast at the Palatine. It was her luxury and she saved up so that we could do it on market day.

Accrington Market was a big brash market, indoors and outdoors, with stalls stacked with dirty potatoes and fat cabbages. There were stalls selling household cleaners out of vats – no packaging, you took your own bottles for bleach and your own tubs for caustic soda. There was a stall that sold nothing but whelks and crabs and eels, and a stall that sold chocolate biscuits in paper bags.

You could get a tattoo or buy a goldfish and you could have your hair trimmed for half the price of a salon. Stallholders shouted their bargains – 'I won't give you one, I won't give you two, I'll give you three for the price of one. What's that, Missus? Seven for the price of two? How many children have you got? Seven? Does your husband know? What's that? It's all his fault. Lucky man. Here you are then and pray for me when I die . . .'

And they demonstrated their goods – 'This will SWE-EEP! This will VAC-UUM. This will clean up the top of the curtains and round the back of the oven . . . it's all in the nozzles. What, Missus? You don't like the look of my nozzle?'

When the first supermarket opened in Accrington nobody went because the prices might be low but they were set. On the markets nothing was set; you haggled for a bargain. That was part of the pleasure, and the pleasure was in the everyday theatre. The stalls were their own shows. Even if you were so poor that you had to wait to buy your food at the very end of the day you could still have a good time down the market. There were people you knew and there was something to watch.

I am not a fan of supermarkets and I hate shopping there, even for things I can't get elsewhere, like cat food and bin bags. A big part of my dislike of them is the loss of vivid life. The dull apathy of existence now isn't just boring jobs and boring TV; it is the loss of vivid life on the streets; the gossip, the encounters, the heaving messy noisy day that made room for everyone, money or not. And if you couldn't afford to heat your house you could go into the market hall. Sooner or later somebody would buy you a cup of tea. That's how it was.

Mrs Winterson didn't like to be seen bargain-hunting – she left that to my dad and took herself to the Palatine caff. She sat opposite me in the fugged-up window, smoking her cigarettes and thinking about my future.

'When you grow up you'll be a missionary.'

'Where will I go?'

'Away from Accrington.'

I don't know why she hated Accrington as much as she did but she did, and yet she didn't leave. When I left it was as though I had relieved her and betrayed her all at once. She longed for me to be free and did everything she could to make sure it never happened.

★

Accrington is not famous for much. It has the world's worst football team – Accrington Stanley – and a large collection of Tiffany glass donated by Joseph Briggs, an Accrington man who did manage to leave, and who made his name and fortune in New York, working for Tiffany.

If bits of New York came to Accrington, then much bigger bits of Accrington went to New York. Among its oddities, Accrington used to make the world's hardest bricks – there is iron ore in the heavy clay, and that gives the bricks their recognisable bright red colour, as well as their remarkable strength.

The bricks are known as the Nori brick because somebody said they were as hard as iron and stamped it on the bricks backwards by mistake – so Nori they became.

Thousands of these bricks went to New York to build the foundations of the 1,454-foot-tall Empire State Building. Think *King Kong* and think Accrington. It was the Nori brick that kept the gorilla swinging Fay Wray. We used to have special showings of *King Kong* at the little cinema in the town and there was always a newsreel about the bricks. Nobody had ever been to New York City, but we all felt personally responsible for its success as the world's most modern city with the world's tallest building standing on Accrington brick.

The famous bricks had a more domestic life too. Walter Gropius, the Bauhaus architect, used Nori bricks for his only residential building in Britain – 66 Old Church Street, Chelsea, London.

Unlike the Empire State Building nobody thought much of Gropius's work but everybody knew about it. We had things to be proud of in Accrington.

The money that came out of the mills and the cotton industry built the market hall and town hall, the Victoria Hospital, the Mechanics' Institute and, later, in part, the public library.

It seems so easy now to destroy libraries – mainly by taking away all the books – and to say that books and libraries are not relevant to people's lives. There's a lot of talk about social breakdown and alienation, but how can it be otherwise when our ideas of progress remove the centres that did so much to keep people together?

In the North people met in the church, in the pub, in the marketplace, and in those philanthropic buildings where they could continue their education and their interests. Now, maybe, the pub is left – but mainly nothing is left.

The library was my door to elsewhere. But there were other doors too – not decorated or municipal, but low and hidden.

There was a second-hand rummage and junk shop somewhere under the viaduct in Accrington which was the last relative of the nineteenth-century rag-and-bone shops. There was a rag-and-bone cart that came round the streets most weeks, and people threw on it what they didn't want and bargained to take home what they did want. I never knew what the man was called, but he had a little Jack Russell terrier called Nip that stood on top of the rag-and-bone cart, barking and guarding the junk.

Under the viaduct was a slam-door of prison-grade steel. Get inside, and you walked down a mummified passage hung with half-dead horsehair mattresses. The Rag Man hung them on meathooks like carcasses, the hooks wedged through the steel springs.

Walk further and the passage broke into a small chamber that wheezed fumes in your face. The wheeze was from a flame heater – a shooting angry jet of gas and fire that the Rag Man used to keep himself warm.

His was the kind of place that sold pre-war prams with wheels the size of millstones and canvas hoods on steel frames. The canvas was mildewed and torn, and sometimes he'd prop a china-head doll under the hood, its glazed eyes malevolent and watchful. He had hundreds of chairs, most with a leg missing like survivors of a shoot-out. He had rusty canary cages and balding stuffed animals, knitted blankets and trolleys on castors. He had tin baths and washboards, clothes mangles and bedpans.

If you fought your way through the Victorian fringed standard lamps and orphaned patchwork quilts, if you crawled under walnut sideboards with their doors off and half-chopped church pews, if you could flatten yourself past the hot dry airless tombs of bedding still tubercular, and sheets hanging like ghosts – the lost linen of lines of the unemployed selling everything and sleeping in sacks – all of that sweated in misery, then, if you could press past and beyond the children's tricycles left with one wheel and the hobby horses without manes and the punctured leather footballs with their dirty criss-cross leather laces, then you came to the books.

ChatterBox Annual, 1923. *The Gollywog News*, 1915. *Empire for Boys*, 1911. *Empire for Girls* . . . *The Astral Plane*, 1913. *How To Keep A Cow. How To Keep A Pig. How To Keep House.*

I loved those – life was so simple – you decided what you wanted to keep – livestock, homestead, wife, bees – and the books told you how to do it. It made for confidence . . .

And in the midst of those things, like the burning bush, were complete sets of Dickens, the Brontës, Sir Walter Scott. They were cheap to buy and I bought them – sloping into the warren of storerooms after work, knowing he'd stay open playing his ancient opera records on one of those radiograms with Bakelite knobs and an arm that moved all on its own to touch down on the black spinning surface of the vinyl.

What is life to me without thee?
What is left if thou art dead?
What is life; life without thee?
What is life without my love?
Eurydice! Eurydice!

It was Kathleen Ferrier singing – the contralto born in Blackburn, five miles from Accrington. The telephonist who had won a singing competition and become as famous as Maria Callas.

Mrs Winterson had heard Kathleen Ferrier sing at Blackburn Town Hall, and she liked to play Kathleen Ferrier songs on the piano. She often sang in her own style that famous aria from Gluck's *Orfeo* – 'What is life to me without thee?'.

We had no time for death. The war plus the Apocalypse plus eternal life made death ridiculous. Death/life. What did it matter as long as you had your soul?

'How many men did you kill, Dad?'

'I don't recall. Twenty. I killed six with my bayonet.

They gave the bullets to the officers – not to us – they said, "We've no bullets, strap on your bayonets."'

The D-Day landings. My dad survived. None of his friends did.

And in the war before, the First World War, Lord Kitchener had decided that men who were friends made better soldiers. Accrington managed to send 720 men – the Accrington Pals – to Serre in France. They trained on the hill at the top of my street and they set off to be heroes. On 1 July 1916 the Battle of the Somme pushed them forward in steady lines that did not waver as the German machine guns took them down. 586 of them were killed or wounded.

In the rag-and-bone shop we sat by the radiogram. The man gave me a poem to read about a dead soldier. He said it was by Wilfred Owen, a young poet killed in 1918. I know the beginning now but I didn't then . . . but I couldn't forget the end . . .

And in his eyes / The cold stars lighting, very old and bleak / In different skies.

I was often out at night – walking home or in lockout on the doorstep – so I spent a lot of time looking at the stars and wondering if they looked the same somewhere that wasn't Accrington.

My mother's eyes were like cold stars. She belonged in a different sky.

Sometimes, when she hadn't been to sleep at all, she'd be there in the morning waiting for the corner shop to open and she'd make an egg custard. Egg-custard mornings made me nervous. When I came home from school nobody would be there – Dad would be at work and she had done a Disappearance. So I used to go round to the back alley and climb over the wall and see if she had left the back door open. Usually she did do that if it was a Disappearance, and the egg custard would be there under a cloth and a bit of money to go to the shop and get a pie.

The only problem was that the doors were locked so it meant climbing over the wall again, returning with the pie and hoping you could get back over without squashing it. Onion and potato for me, meat and onion for Dad when he came home.

At the corner shop they always knew she had Disappeared.

'She'll be back tomorrow, will Connie. She always comes back.'

That was true. She always came back. I never asked her where she went and I still don't know. I never eat egg custard either.

There were so many corner shops in Accrington. People opened them in their front rooms and lived upstairs. There were bread shops and pie shops and vegetable shops and shops that sold sweets in jars.

The best sweet shop was run by two ladies who may or may not have been lovers. One was quite young, but the older one wore a woollen balaclava all the time – not the full-face version, but a balaclava nonetheless. And she had a moustache. But a lot of women had moustaches in those days. I never met anybody who shaved anything, and it didn't occur to me to shave anything myself until I turned up at Oxford looking like a werewolf.

But I suspect that my mother had seen *The Killing of Sister George* (1968), where Beryl Reid plays a bawling brassy butch dyke sadistically tormenting her younger blonde girlfriend called Childie. It is a magnificent and unsettling movie but not one likely to win Mrs W over to the cause of gay rights.

She loved going to the pictures, even though it was not allowed and even though she couldn't afford it. Whenever we passed by the Odeon Cinema she looked carefully at the posters, and sometimes, when she went on one of her Disappearances, I think she was at the Odeon.

Whatever the truth of the story, there came a day when I was forbidden to go into the sweet shop. This was a blow because I always got extra jelly babies from them. When I pestered Mrs Winterson about it she said they dealt in unnatural passions. At the time I assumed this meant they put chemicals in their sweets.

My other favourite shops, also forbidden, were the selling-out shops, now called off-licences, where women in headscarves took string bags to buy bottles of stout.

Although they were forbidden, these were the places where Mrs W got her cigarettes, and quite often she sent me, saying, 'Tell them they're for your dad.'

All the booze bottles were returnable and carried a deposit in those days, and I soon worked out that the returns were kept in crates round the back and it was easy to pull a couple out and 'return' them again.

The selling-out shops were full of men and women who swore and talked about sex and betting on greyhounds, so all that plus free money and being forbidden made it very exciting.

When I think about it now I wonder why it was all right for me to go into the selling-out shops and buy cigarettes but all wrong for me to get extra sweets from a couple of women who were happy together, even if one of them wore a balaclava all the time.

I think Mrs Winterson was afraid of happiness. Jesus was supposed to make you happy but he didn't, and if you were waiting for the Apocalypse that never came, you were bound to feel disappointed.

She thought that happy meant bad/wrong/sinful. Or plain stupid. Unhappy seemed to have virtue attached to it.

But there were exceptions. The Gospel Tent was an exception, and Royal Albert was an exception, and so was Christmas. She loved Christmas.

In Accrington there was always a huge tree outside the market hall, and the Salvation Army played carols there for most of December.

At Christmas time the bartering system was in full swing. We could offer Brussels spouts on stalks from our allotment, apples wrapped in newspaper to make sauce, and best of all the once-a-year cherry brandy made from the morello cherry tree in the yard, and steeped half a year in the back of a cupboard on the way to Narnia.

We swapped our goods for smoked eel, crunchy like grated glass, and for a pudding made in cloth – a pudding made the proper way, and hard like a cannonball and speckled with fruit like a giant bird's egg. It stayed in slices when you cut it, and we poured the cherry brandy over the top and set it on fire, my dad turning the light out while my mother carried it into the parlour.

The flames lit up her face. The coal fire lit up me and my dad. We were happy.

On 21 December every year my mother went out in her hat and coat – she wouldn't say where – while my father and I strung paperchains, made by me, from the corners of the parlour cornice to the centre light. My mother returned, in what seemed to be a hailstorm, though maybe that was her personal weather. She carried a goose half in, half out of her bag, its slack head hung sideways like a dream nobody could remember. She gave it to me, goose and dream, and I plucked the feathers into a bucket. We kept the feathers to restuff whatever needed restuffing and we saved the thick goose fat we drained from the bird for roasting potatoes through the winter. Apart from Mrs W who had a thyroid problem everybody we knew was as thin as a ferret. We needed goose fat.

Christmas was the one time of the year when my mother went out into the world looking as though the world was more than a Vale of Tears.

She got dressed up and came to my school concerts – and that meant wearing her mother's fur coat and a half-hat made of black feathers. Hat and coat were circa 1940 and this was in the 1970s, but she cut a dash, and she always had good posture, and as the whole of the North was in the wrong decade until the 1980s, nobody noticed.

The concerts were extremely ambitious; the first half was something daunting like the Fauré *Requiem* or the *St Anthony Chorale*, and it required the full power of the choir and orchestra and usually a soloist or two from the Hallé Orchestra in Manchester.

We had a music teacher who played the cello with

the Halle, and she was one of those electrical trapped women of a particular generation who are half mad because they are trapped, and half genius because they are trapped. She wanted her girls to know about music – to sing it, to play it, and to make no compromises.

We were terrified of her. If she was playing the piano at school assembly, she would play Rachmaninov, her hair dark over the Steinway, her fingernails always red.

The school song at Accrington High School for Girls was 'Let Us Now Praise Famous Men', a terrible choice for an all-girls' school, but one that helped turn me into a feminist. Where were the famous women – indeed any women – and why weren't we praising them? I vowed to myself that I would be famous and that I would come back and be praised.

That seemed very unlikely as I was a terrible pupil, inattentive and troublesome, and my reports were year-in year-out awful. I couldn't concentrate and I didn't understand much of what was being said to me.

I was only good at one thing: words. I had read more, much more, than anybody else, and I knew how words worked in the way that some boys knew how engines worked.

But it was Christmas and the school was lit up and Mrs Winterson was in her fur coat and bird hat and my dad was washed and shaved and I was walking in between them and it felt normal.

'Is that your mum?' said somebody.

'Mostly,' I said.

★

Years later, when I came back to Accrington after my first term at Oxford, it was snowing and I was walking up the long stretchy street from the train station, counting the lamp posts. I got near 200 Water Street and heard her before I saw her, her back to the window onto the street, very upright, very big, playing her new electronic organ – 'In the Bleak Midwinter', with a jazz riff and cymbals.

I looked at her through the window. It had always been through the window – there was a barrier between us, transparent but real – but it says in the Bible, doesn't it, that we see through a glass darkly?

She was my mother. She wasn't my mother.

I rang the bell. She half turned. 'Come in, come in, the door's open.'

8

The Apocalypse

M RS WINTERSON WAS NOT A welcoming woman. If anyone knocked at the door she ran down the lobby and shoved the poker through the letter box.

I reminded her that angels often come in disguise and she said that was true but they didn't come disguised in Crimplene.

Part of the problem was that we had no bathroom and she was ashamed of this. Not many people did have bathrooms but I was not allowed to have friends from school in case they wanted to use the toilet – and then they would have to go outside – and then they would discover that we had no bathroom.

In fact, that was the least of it. A bigger challenge for unbelievers than a draughty encounter with an outside loo was what was waiting for them when they got there.

We were not allowed books but we lived in a world of print. Mrs Winterson wrote out exhortations and stuck them all over the house.

Under my coat peg a sign said THINK OF GOD NOT THE DOG.

Over the gas oven, on a loaf wrapper, it said MAN SHALL NOT LIVE BY BREAD ALONE.

But in the outside loo, directly in front of you as you went through the door, was a placard. Those who stood up read LINGER NOT AT THE LORD'S BUSINESS.

Those who sat down read HE SHALL MELT THY BOWELS LIKE WAX.

This was wishful thinking; my mother was having trouble with her bowels. It was something to do with the loaf of white sliced we couldn't live by.

When I went to school my mother put quotes from the Scriptures in my hockey boots. At mealtimes there was a little scroll from the Promise Box by each of our plates. A Promise Box is a box with Bible texts rolled up in it, like the jokes you get in Christmas crackers, but serious. The little rolls stand on end and you close your eyes and pick one out. It can be comforting: LET NOT YOUR HEARTS BE TROUBLED NEITHER LET THEM BE AFRAID. Or it can be frightening: THE SINS OF THE FATHERS SHALL BE VISITED ON THE CHILDREN.

But cheery or depressing, it was all reading and reading was what I wanted to do. Fed words and shod with them, words became clues. Piece by piece I knew they would lead me somewhere else.

The only time that Mrs Winterson liked to answer the door was when she knew that the Mormons were coming round. Then she waited in the lobby, and before they had dropped the knocker she had flung open the door waving her Bible and warning them of eternal damnation. This was confusing for the Mormons because they thought they were in charge of eternal damnation. But Mrs Winterson was a better candidate for the job.

Now and again, if she was in a sociable frame of mind and there was a knock at the door, she left the poker alone and sent me out the back door to run up the alley and peer round the corner down the street to see who was there. I ran back with the news and then she decided whether or not they could come in – this usually meant a lot of work with the fly-spray air freshener while I went to open the door. By now, discouraged by no response, the visitor would be halfway down the street so I had to run and fetch them back, and then my mother would pretend to be surprised and pleased.

I didn't care; it gave me a chance to go upstairs and read a forbidden book.

I think Mrs Winterson had been well read at one time. When I was about seven she read *Jane Eyre* to me. This was deemed suitable because it has a minister in it – St John Rivers – who is keen on missionary work.

Mrs Winterson read out loud, turning the pages. There is the terrible fire at Thornfield Hall and Mr Rochester goes blind, but in the version Mrs Winterson read, Jane doesn't bother about her now sightless paramour; she marries St John Rivers and they go off together to work in the mission field. It was only when I finally read *Jane Eyre* for myself that I found out what my mother had done.

And she did it so well, turning the pages and inventing the text extempore in the style of Charlotte Brontë.

The book disappeared as I got older – perhaps she didn't want me to read it for myself.

I assumed that she hid books the way she hid

everything else, including her heart, but our house was small and I searched it. Were we endlessly ransacking the house, the two of us, looking for evidence of each other? I think we were – she, because I was fatally unknown to her, and she was afraid of me. Me, because I had no idea what was missing but felt the missing-ness of the missing.

We circled each other, wary, abandoned, full of longing. We came close but not close enough and then we pushed each other away forever.

I did find a book, but I wish I hadn't; it was hidden in the tallboy under a pile of flannels, and it was a 1950s sex manual called *How to Please Your Husband*.

This terrifying tome might have explained why Mrs Winterson didn't have children. It had black-and-white diagrams and lists and tips and most of the positions looked like adverts for a children's game of physical torment called Twister.

As I pondered the horrors of heterosexuality I realised that I need not feel sorry for either of my parents; my mother hadn't read it – perhaps she had opened it once, realised the extent of the task, and put it away. The book was flat, pristine, intact. So whatever my father had had to do without, and I really don't think they ever had sex, he hadn't had to spend his nights with Mrs W with one hand on his penis and the other holding the manual while she followed the instructions.

I remember her telling me that soon after they were married my father had come home drunk and she had locked him out of the bedroom. He had broken down the door and she had thrown her wedding ring out of the window and into the gutter. He went to find it. She got the night bus to Blackburn. This was offered as an illustration of how Jesus improves a marriage.

The only sex education my mother ever gave me was the injunction: 'Never let a boy touch you *down there.*' I had no idea what she meant. She seemed to be referring to my knees.

Would it have been better if I had fallen for a boy and not a girl? Probably not. I had entered her own fearful place – the terror of the body, the irresolution of her marriage, her own mother's humiliation at her father's coarseness and womanising. Sex disgusted her. And now, when she saw me, she saw sex.

I had made my promises. And in any case Helen had gone away. But now I was someone who wanted to be naked with someone else. I was someone who had loved the feel of skin, of sweat, of kissing, of coming. I wanted sex and I wanted closeness.

Inevitably there would be another lover. She knew that. She was watching me. Inevitably she forced it to happen.

I had finished my O levels and done pretty badly. I failed four, got five, and my school had closed down, or rather it had become a comprehensive school without a sixth form. That was part of the Labour government's education policy. I was able to go on to a techanical college to take my A levels, and with some grumbling Mrs Winterson had agreed, providing I worked on the markets in the evenings and on Saturday to bring some money into the house.

I was glad to get out of the school and make a

fresh start. Nobody thought I would come to much. The burning place inside me seemed like anger and trouble to them. They didn't know how many books I had read or what I was writing up in the hills on long days alone. On the top of the hill looking out over the town I wanted to see further than anybody had seen. That wasn't arrogance; it was desire. I was all desire, desire for life.

And I was lonely.

Mrs Winterson had succeeded there; her own loneliness, impossible to breach, had begun to wall us all in.

It was summer and it was time for the annual holiday in Blackpool.

This holiday consisted of a coach ride to the famous seaside town and a week in a backstreet boarding house – we couldn't afford a sea view. My mother sat in a deckchair most of the day reading sensationalist literature about Hell, and my father walked about. He loved walking.

In the evenings we all went gambling on the slot machines. This was not deemed to be gambling proper. If we won, we got fish and chips.

When I was a child I was happy with all of this and I think they were happy too, in that brief, carefree, once-a-year one-week holiday. But our lives had got darker. Since the exorcism the year before we had all been ill.

My mother started staying in bed all day for days on end, making my dad sleep downstairs because she said she was vomiting.

Then she had manic sessions when she stayed up

all day and all night, knitting, baking, listening to the radio. Dad went to work – he had no choice – but he stopped making things. He used to make clay animals and fire them in the kiln at work. Now he hardly spoke. No one spoke. And it was time to go on holiday.

My periods had stopped. I had had glandular fever and I was exhausted. I liked being at the technical college and working the markets, but I was sleeping ten hours a night every night, and it was the first time, but not the last, that I could hear voices, quite clearly, that were not inside my head. That is, they presented themselves as outside my head.

I asked to stay at home.

My mother said nothing.

On the morning of departure my mother packed the two suitcases, one for my dad and one for herself, and they left the house. I walked down the street with them to the coach station. I asked for the house key.

She said she couldn't trust me in the house on my own. I could stay with the pastor. It had been arranged.

'You didn't tell me.'

'I'm telling you now.'

The coach pulled in. People started getting on.

'Give me the key. I live there.'

'We'll be back next Saturday.'

'Dad . . .'

'You heard what Connie said . . .'

They got on the coach.

I had been seeing a girl who was still at the school – I have a late August birthday so I was always the youngest in my year. This girl Janey had an October

106

birthday so she was one of the oldest – we were a year apart academically but only a couple of months in age. She was coming to the college in the autumn. I liked her a lot, but I was too scared to kiss her. She was popular with the boys and had a boyfriend. But it was me she wanted to see.

I went round to her house and told her what had happened and her mother, who was a decent woman, let me sleep in their caravan parked outside the house.

I was filled with rage. We went for a walk and I pulled a farm gate off its hinges and threw it into the river. Janey put her arm round me. 'Let's go and break in. It's your house.'

So that night we climbed over the back wall and into the yard. My dad kept a few tools in a little shed and I found a jemmy bar and a claw hammer and prised open the kitchen door.

We were in.

We were like kids. We *were* kids. We heated up a Fray Bentos steak pie – they used to be sold in flat saucer-shaped tins – and we opened some canned peas. There was a canning factory in our town and tins of food were cheap.

We drank some of the bottled stuff everybody loved called sarsparilla – it tasted like liquorice and treacle and it was black and fizzy and sold in unlabelled bottles from a market stall. I always bought it when I had the money, and I bought it for Mrs Winterson too.

The house was looking nice. Mrs Winterson had been decorating. She was expert at measuring and putting up wallpaper. My dad's job was to mix the paste, cut the lengths of wallpaper to her directions, then pass the sheets up the ladder so that she could drop and hang them and dust out the air bubbles with her big brush.

Naturally, the operation had her signature-style on it. As a compulsive-obsessive it had to be done until it was done.

I came home. She was up the ladder singing 'Will Your Anchor Hold in the Storms of Life'.

My dad wanted his tea because he had to go to work, but that was all right because it was ready and in the oven.

'Are you coming down, Connie?'

'Not till I'm done.'

My dad and me sat in the living room eating our mince and potatoes in silence. Above us was the *whisk whisk* of the wallpaper brush.

'Do you not want something to eat, Connie?'

'Don't mind me. I'll just have a sandwich up the ladder.'

So the sandwich had to be made and brought to her and passed up like feeding a dangerous animal in a safari park. She sat there, with her scarf on to keep bits out of her perm, her head just at ceiling height, eating her sandwich and looking down at us.

Dad went off to work. The ladder moved round the room a bit but she was still up it. I went off to bed and when I got up for college the next morning, there she was, with a cup of tea, up the ladder.

Had she been there all night? Had she got back up when she heard me coming down?

But the living room was decorated.

Janey and I were both dark-eyed intense types though she laughed more than I did. Her dad had a good job but there was a worry that he would lose it. Her mother worked and there were four children. She was the eldest. If her dad did lose his job she would have to give up college and start work.

Everybody we knew used cash and when you had no cash you had no money. Borrowing money was seen as the road to ruin. When my father died in 2008 he had never had a credit or debit card. He had a building society account for savings only.

Janey knew that her dad had a loan and that a man came round for the money every Friday. She was frightened of the man.

I told her not to be frightened. I said there would be a time when we would never be frightened again.

We held hands. I was wondering what it would be like to have a home of your own where you could come and go, where people would be welcome, where you would never be frightened again . . .

We heard the front door open. There were dogs barking. The door into the living room was shoved open. Two Dobermanns ran in growling and pawing and backing up. Janey screamed.

Behind the Dobermanns was my mother's brother – Uncle Alec.

Mrs Winterson had decided that I would come back to the house. She knew I would climb over the back wall. She had paid a neighbour to telephone her at the boarding house in Blackpool. The neighbour had spotted me, gone round to the phone box, phoned Blackpool, and spoken to my mother. My mother telephoned her brother.

She loathed him. There was nothing between them

but loathing. He had inherited the motor business from their father, and she had been left with nothing. All the nursing of her mother, all the years of looking after Grandad, cooking his meals, washing his clothes, had left her with nothing but a miserable house and no money. Her brother had a thriving garage and petrol station.

He told me to get out. I said I wouldn't go. He said I'd go if he had to set the dogs on me. He meant it. He told me I was ungrateful.

'I said to Connie don't go adopting. You don't know what you get.'

'Drop dead.'

'You what?'

'Drop dead.'

Slam. Straight across the face. Janey was really crying now. I had a split lip. Uncle Alec was flushed, furious.

'I'll give you five minutes and I'll be back in here and you'll wish you'd never been born.'

But I have never wished that and I wasn't going to start wishing it for him.

He went out and I heard him get in his car and start the engine. I could hear it running. I ran upstairs and got some clothes, then I went into the War Cupboard and pulled out a load of tinned food. Janey put it all in her bag.

We went back out over the wall so that he wouldn't see us. Let him storm in again after his five minutes were up and shout at nothing.

I felt cold inside. I felt nothing inside. I could have killed him. I would have killed him. I would have killed him and felt nothing.

★

At Janey's her parents had gone out and her grandma was babysitting. The boys had gone to bed. I was sitting on the floor of the caravan. Janey came and put her arms round me, then she kissed me, really kissed me.

I was crying then, and kissing her, and we got undressed and into the little caravan bed, and I remembered, my body remembered, what it was like to be in one place and to be able to be there – not watchful, not worried, not with your head somewhere else.

Did we fall asleep? We must have done. There were the car headlights sweeping across the caravan. Her parents were coming home. I felt my heart beating too fast, but the lights were not a warning. We were safe. We were together.

She had beautiful breasts. She was all beautiful, with a rich thick triangle of black hair at the fork of her legs, and dark hair on her arms and in a line from her belly to her pubic hair.

In the morning when we woke early she said, 'I love you. I've loved you for ages.'

'I was too scared,' I said.

'Don't be,' she said. 'Not any more.'

And her clearness was like water, cool and deep and see-through right to the bottom. No guilt. No fear.

She told her mother about us, and her mother warned her not to tell her father, or to let him find out.

We took our bicycles. We went twenty miles and made love under a hedge. Janey's hand was covered in blood. My periods had started again.

The next day we cycled to Blackpool. I went to

my mother and asked her why she had done it. Why
had she locked me out? Why didn't she trust me? I
didn't ask her why she no longer loved me. Love was
not a word that could be used between us any more.
It was not a simple do you?/don't you? Love was not
an emotion; it was the bomb site between us.

She looked at Janey. She looked at me. She said,
'You're no daughter of mine.'

It hardly mattered. It was too late for lines like
that now. I had a language of my own and it wasn't
hers.

Janey and I were happy. We went to college. We
saw each other every day. I had started driving lessons
in a beat-up Mini on a piece of spare land. I was
living in my own world of books and love. The world
was vivid and untouched. I felt free again – I think
because I was loved. I took Mrs Winterson some
flowers.

When I got back that night, the flowers were in a
vase on the table. I looked at them . . . The stalks of
the flowers were in the vase. She had cut off the heads
and thrown them on the unlit fire. The fire was ready-
laid, and on the neat black layer of coal were the
white heads of the little carnations.

My mother was sitting silently in the chair. I said
nothing. I looked at the room, small and spruce, at
the brass flying ducks over the mantelpiece, at the
brass crocodile nutcracker next to the mantel clock,
at the clothes rack that we could raise and lower over
the fire, at the sideboard with our photographs on it.
This is where I lived.

She said, 'It's no good. I know what you are.'

'I don't think you do.'

'Touching her. Kissing her. Naked. In bed together. Do you think I don't know what you're doing?'

All right . . . this was it . . . no hiding this time. No second self. No secrets.

'Mum . . . I love Janey.'

'So you're all over her . . . hot bodies, hands everywhere . . .'

'I love her.'

'I gave you a chance. You're back with the Devil. So I tell you now, either you get out of this house and you don't come back or you stop seeing that girl. I'm going to tell her mother.'

'She knows.'

'She what?'

'Her mother knows. She's not like you.'

Mrs Winterson was quiet for a long time and then she started to cry. 'It's a sin. You'll be in Hell. Soft bodies all the way to Hell.'

I went upstairs and started packing my things. I had no idea what I was going to do.

When I came down my mother was sitting stock-still staring into space.

'I'll go then . . .' I said.

She didn't answer. I left the room. I walked down the dark narrow lobby, the coats on their pegs. Nothing to say. I was at the front door. I heard her behind me. I turned.

'Jeanette, will you tell me why?'

'What why?'

'You know what why . . .'

But I don't know what why . . . what I am . . . why I don't please her. What she wants. Why I am not what she wants. What I want or why. But there is something I know: 'When I am with her I am happy. Just happy.'

She nodded. She seemed to understand and I thought, really, for that second, that she would change her mind, that we would talk, that we would be on the same side of the glass wall. I waited.

She said, 'Why be happy when you could be normal?'

9

English Literature A–Z

THE ACCRINGTON PUBLIC LIBRARY HAD a copy of most things. It had a copy of Gertrude Stein's *The Autobiography of Alice B. Toklas* (1932).

When I was sixteen I had only got as far as M – not counting Shakespeare, who is not part of the alphabet, any more than black is a colour. Black is all the colours and Shakespeare is all the alphabet. I was reading his plays and sonnets the way that you get dressed every morning. You don't ask yourself, 'Shall I get dressed today?' (On the days you don't get dressed you are not well enough, either mentally or physically, to be able to ask – but we will go there later.)

M was the seventeenth-century poet, Andrew Marvell. After my encounter with T. S. Eliot on the library steps, I had decided to add poetry to the reading list. Poetry is easier to learn than prose. Once you have learned it you can use it as a light and a laser. It shows up your true situation and it helps you cut through it.

Marvell wrote one of the most wonderful poems in English – 'To His Coy Mistress'. That's the one that begins: *Had we but world enough, and time . . .*

World enough, and time: I was young, so I had time, but I knew I had to find world – I didn't even have a room of my own.

115

What gave me great hope were the closing lines of the poem. It is a seduction poem, which is its charm, but it is also a life poem, urging and celebrating love and desire and declaring desire as a challenge to mortality itself.

We can't slow time, says Marvell, but we can chase it. We can make time run. Think of the hourglass, the cliché of the sands of time slowly dribbling away, and all those Faust-like wishes of immortality – if only time could stop, if only we could live forever.

No, says Marvell, forget that, turn it round, live it out as exuberantly as you can. Here he is, much better than me:

> Let us roll all our strength and all
> Our sweetness up into one ball;
> And tear our pleasures with rough strife
> Thorough the iron gates of life.
> Thus, though we cannot make our sun
> Stand still, yet we will make him run.

Read it aloud. And look what Marvell makes happen by putting the line break at 'sun'. The line break right there forces a nano-pause, and so the sun does indeed stand still – then the line gallops forward.

I thought, 'If I can't stay where I am, and I can't, then I will put all that I can into the going.'

I began to realise that I had company. Writers are often exiles, outsiders, runaways and castaways. These writers were my friends. Every book was a message in a bottle. Open it.

★

M. Katherine Mansfield – the only writer Virginia Woolf envied . . . but I had not read Virginia Woolf.

In any case, I did not think in terms of gender or feminism, not then, because I had no wider politics other than knowing I was working class. But I had noticed that the women were fewer and further apart on the shelves, and when I tried to read books 'about' literature (always a mistake), I couldn't help noticing that the books were written by men about men who write.

That didn't worry me; I was in danger of drowning and nobody lost at sea worries about whether the spar they cling to is made of elm or oak.

Katherine Mansfield – another tubercular writer like Lawrence and Keats, and they all made me feel better about my non-stop cough. Katherine Mansfield – a writer whose short stories are as far away from any life experience I had had at sixteen.

But that was the point. Reading things that are relevant to the facts of your life is of limited value. The facts are, after all, only the facts, and the yearning passionate part of you will not be met there. That is why reading ourselves as a fiction as well as fact is so liberating. The wider we read the freer we become. Emily Dickinson barely left her homestead in Amherst, Massachusetts, but when we read, 'My life stood – a loaded gun' we know we have met an imagination that will detonate life, not decorate it.

So I read on. And I read on, past my own geography and history, past the foundling stories and the Nori brickworks, past the Devil and the wrong crib. The great writers were not remote; they were in Accrington.

★

The Accrington Public Library ran on the Dewey decimal system, which meant that books were meticulously catalogued, except for Pulp Fiction which everybody despised. So Romance was just given a pink strip and all Romance was simply chucked unalphabetically onto the Romance shelves. Sea Stories were treated the same way, but with a green strip. Horror had a black strip. Mystery stories shlock-style had a white strip, but the librarian would never file Chandler or Highsmith under Mystery – they were literature, just as *Moby-Dick* was not a Sea Story and *Jane Eyre* was not Romance.

Humour had a section too . . . with a wavy orange giggle strip. On the Humour shelves, I will never know why or how, was Gertrude Stein, presumably because she wrote what looked like nonsense . . .

Well, maybe she did, and often she did, though for reasons that made a lot of sense, but *The Autobiography of Alice B. Toklas* is a delightful book, and a true groundbreaking moment in English literature – in the same way that Virginia Woolf's *Orlando* (1928) is groundbreaking.

Woolf called her novel a biography, and Stein wrote somebody else's autobiography. Both women were collapsing the space between fact and fiction – *Orlando* used the real-life Vita Sackville-West as its heroine, and Stein used her lover, Alice B. Toklas.

Sure, Defoe had called *Robinson Crusoe* an autobiography (Stein references that), and Charlotte Brontë had to call *Jane Eyre* a biography, because women were not supposed to go around making things up – especially stories where the morality is daring if not dodgy.

But Woolf and Stein were radical to use real people in their fictions and to muddle their facts – *Orlando*, with its actual photos of Vita Sackville-West, and Alice Toklas, the supposed writer, who is Stein's lover but not the writer . . .

For me, fascinated with identity, and how you define yourself, those books were crucial. Reading yourself as a fiction as well as a fact is the only way to keep the narrative open – the only way to stop the story running away under its own momentum, often towards an ending no one wants.

The night I left home I felt that I had been tricked or trapped into going – and not even by Mrs Winterson, but by the dark narrative of our life together.

Her fatalism was so powerful. She was her own black hole that pulled in all the light. She was made of dark matter and her force was invisible, unseen except in its effects.

What would it have meant to be happy? What would it have meant if things had been bright, clear, good between us?

It was never a question of biology or nature and nurture. I know now that we heal up through being loved, and through loving others. We don't heal by forming a secret society of one – by obsessing about the only other 'one' we might admit, and being doomed to disappointment. Mrs Winterson was her own secret society, and she longed for me to join her there. It was a compulsive doctrine, and I carried it forward in my own life for a long time. It is of course the basis of romantic love – you + me against the world. A world where there are only two of us. A world that doesn't really exist, except that we are in it. And when one of us fails the other . . .

And one of us will always fail the other.

When I walked away that night I was longing for love and loyalty. The wide yearning of my nature had to funnel through a narrow neck – it went into the idea of the 'other', the almost-twin, who would be so near to me but not me. A Plato-like split of a complete being. We would find each other one day – and then everything would be all right.

I had to believe that – how else would I have coped? And yet I was heading for the dangerous losses that 'all or nothing' love demands.

But – and this matters – you really don't have much choice when you are sixteen. You leave with your inheritance.

But . . .

There is always a wild card. And what I had were books. What I had, most of all, was the language that books allowed. A way to talk about complexity. A way to '*keep the heart awake to love and beauty*' (Coleridge).

I walked around for most of the night the night that I left home. The night was in slow motion, and nights are so much slower than days. Time is not constant and one minute is not the same length as another.

I was in a night that was lengthening into my life. I walked away and I was trying to walk away from the dark orbit of her depression. I was trying to walk out of the shadow she cast. I wasn't really going anywhere. I was going to be away, free, or so it seemed, but you always take it with you. It takes much longer to leave the psychic place than the physical place.

I slept in the shelters on the bowling green between about 4 a.m. and 6 a.m. and woke freezing and stiff to the cloud-broken light of October. I went down to the market and bought fried eggs and strong tea, and then took my few things to college with me.

The next few days were difficult. Janey's father had decided that he really didn't like me – I had that effect on my friends' parents – and so I couldn't sleep in the caravan. Instead, I slept in the beaten-up old Mini that I was learning to drive.

It was a very good Mini, and it belonged to a crazy boy at church whose parents were elderly, not religious, but doting. He let me use it because they wanted him to have his own car and he was terrified of driving. Between us we drove it over to Janey's house and parked it round the corner.

The only way to sleep in a car is to have a plan. Mine was to sit in the front to read and eat and to lie down in the back to sleep. That way I felt like I was in control. I kept my stuff in the boot, and after a few days I decided to start driving the Mini around town, even though I didn't have a licence.

I was working on the market packing up jumpers three evenings a week and on Saturdays from 8 a.m. to 6 p.m. I worked on a fruit and veg stall, so I had money for food, petrol and the launderette.

Every Saturday Janey and I went to the pictures, ate fish and chips, and made love in the back of the Mini. Then she went home and I went to sleep reading Nabokov by flashlight. I was not happy about reaching N.

I couldn't understand why a man should find the mature female body so disgusting. The best thing about taking my showers at the public baths was being able to look at women. I found them beautiful, all of them. And that in itself was a rebuke to my mother who only understood bodies as sinful and ugly.

Looking at women was not really sexual for me. I loved Janey and she was sexual, but looking at women was a way of looking at myself and, I suppose, a way of loving myself. I don't know how it would have been if I had wanted boys, but I didn't. I liked some of them but I didn't desire any of them. Not then. Not yet.

One day, when I got to my sixth-form college, and we were reading Wilfred Owen and *Middlemarch* for the exam, I complained about Nabokov. I found *Lolita* upsetting. This was the first time that literature felt like a betrayal. I had asked the librarian – usually reliable – and she said that she disliked Nabokov too, and that many women felt that way but it was better not to say so in mixed company.

Men will call you provincial, she said, and I asked what that meant, and she explained that it meant someone who came from the provinces. I asked her if Accrington was the provinces, but she said, no, it was beyond the provinces.

So I decided to ask my teachers.

I had two English teachers. The main one was a sexy wildman who eventually married one of our classmates when she managed to turn eighteen. He said that Nabokov was truly great and that one day I would understand that. 'He hates women,' I said, not realising that this was the beginning of my feminism.

'He hates what women become,' said the wildman. 'That's different. He loves women until they become what they become.'

And then we had an argument about Dorothea Brook in *Middlemarch*, and the revolting Rosamund, whom all the men prefer, presumably because she hasn't become what women become . . .

The argument led nowhere and I went trampolining with a couple of girls who weren't worried about Dorothea Brook or Lolita. They just liked trampolining.

We were making so much noise on our trampoline that we disturbed the head of English, Mrs Ratlow.

Mrs Ratlow was a middle-aged lady, round-shaped like a fluffy cat. She had fluffy hair and purple eye make-up. She wore red polyester suits and green frilly blouses. She was vain and frightening and ridiculous all at once, and we were either laughing at her or hiding from her. But she loved literature. Whenever she said 'Shakespeare', she bowed her head, and she had actually taken the coach to Stratford-upon-Avon in 1970 to see Peter Brook's legendary white-box production of *A Midsummer Night's Dream*. She was a kind of Miss Jean Brodie I suppose, though I didn't suppose because I hadn't got as far as S, and when I did get there, there was no Muriel Spark. Too modern for English Literature in Prose A–Z.

But there was Mrs Ratlow – widowed with two teenage sons who towered over her and who always arrived at the college in a hail of threats from Mrs Ratlow as she drove into the car park and shoehorned the huge hulking boys out of her tiny Riley Elf. She shouted all the time. She took Valium in class.

She threw books at our heads and she threatened to kill us. All of that was still allowed.

Mrs Ratlow came tearing out of the English course-work room, foolishly situated by the trampoline room. When she had stopped shouting at us I said it was all to do with Nabokov, and I had to get past N.

'But you're already reading Wilfred Owen.'

'I know, but he's poetry. English Literature in Prose A–Z is what I'm doing. There's a writer called Mrs Oliphant . . .'

Mrs Ratlow puffed up her chest like a pigeon. 'Mrs Oliphant is not literature – you may not read her!'

'I've got no choice – she's on the shelf.'

'Explain yourself, girl,' said Mrs Ratlow, who was interested now in spite of wanting to mark twenty essays on *Pride and Prejudice*.

And so it all came tumbling out – the mother, the Mini, the library, the books. Mrs Ratlow was silent, which was very unusual. Then she said, 'You are living in a Mini and when you are not, in fact, in the Mini, you are working on the market to earn money, or you are here at the college, and otherwise you are in the Accrington Public Library reading English Literature in Prose A–Z.'

Yes, that was an accurate summary of my entire life apart from sex.

'I have now included poetry,' I said, explaining about T. S. Eliot.

She was looking at me like a scene from *Quatermass and the Pit*, as a previously knowable object was transforming in front of her eyes. Then she said, 'There is a spare room in my house. Pay for your own food and no noise after 10 p.m. You can have a key.'

'A key?'

'Yes. A key is a metal device that opens a door.'

I was back to moron-status in her eyes, but I didn't care. I said, 'I have never had a key, except to the Mini.'

'I shall go and speak to that mother of yours.'

'Don't,' I said. 'Please don't.'

She handed me the key. 'Don't expect any lifts into college. The boys sit in the back and my bag sits in the front.' Then she paused, and she said, 'Nabokov may or may not be a great writer. I do not know and I do not care.'

'Do I have to finish *Lolita*?'

'Yes. But you must not read Mrs Oliphant. I shall certainly have a word with the librarian at the weekend. And, in any case, you don't have to read alphabetically, you know.'

I started to say that I had to have an order – like only eating and reading in the front of the Mini and only sleeping in the back – but then I just stopped, just stopped dead, because trampolining had started again and Mrs Ratlow was already firing herself forward towards the sweaty springy bouncing canvas, shouting about Jane Austen.

I went off down to the library with the little silver key in my pocket.

I was helping the librarian shelve the books, something I really liked to do because I liked the weight of the books and the way they slotted onto the shelves.

She gave me a pile of orange giggle-strip Humour, and that is when I first noticed Gertrude Stein.

'I thought you were on N?' said the librarian, who like most librarians believed in alphabetical order.

'I am, but I am having a little look around too,' I said. 'My English teacher told me to do that. She says that Mrs Oliphant is not literature. She's coming to see you about her.'

The librarian raised her eyebrows. 'Is she now? I do not say that I disagree with her. But can we really leap from N to P? Yet, there are difficulties with the letter O.'

'There were difficulties with the letter N.'

'Yes. English literature – perhaps all literature – is never what we expect. And not always what we enjoy. I myself had great difficulties with the letter C . . . Lewis Carroll. Joseph Conrad. Coleridge.'

It was always a mistake to argue with the librarian but before I could stop myself I started to recite:

It were a vain endeavour,
Though I should gaze forever
On that green light that lingers in the west;
I may not hope from outward forms to win
The passion and the life, whose fountains are within.

The librarian regarded me. 'That is very beautiful.'

'It's Coleridge. "Dejection: An Ode".'

'Well, perhaps I shall have to reconsider the letter C.'

'Will I have to reconsider the letter N?'

'My advice is this. When you are young and you read something that you very much dislike, put it aside and read it again three years later. And if you still dislike it, read it again in a further three years. And when you are no longer young – when you are fifty, as am I – read the thing again that you disliked most of all.'

'That'll be *Lolita* then.'

She smiled, which was unusual, so I said, 'Shall I skip Mrs Oliphant?'

'I think you might . . . although she did write a very good ghost story called *The Open Door*.'

I picked up my pile of books for shelving. The library was quiet. It was busy but it was quiet and I thought it must be like this in a monastery where you had company and sympathy but your thoughts were your own. I looked up at the enormous stained-glass window and the beautiful oak staircase. I loved that building.

The librarian was explaining the benefits of the Dewey decimal system to her junior – benefits that extended to every area of life. It was orderly, like the universe. It had logic. It was dependable. Using it allowed a kind of moral uplift, as one's own chaos was also brought under control.

'Whenever I am troubled,' said the librarian, 'I think about the Dewey decimal system.'

'Then what happens?' asked the junior, rather overawed.

'Then I understand that trouble is just something that has been filed in the wrong place. That is what Jung was explaining of course – as the chaos of our unconscious contents strive to find their rightful place in the index of consciousness.'

The junior was silent. I said, 'Who is Jung?'

'That is not for now,' said the librarian. 'And in any case not English Literature A–Z. You would have to go to Psychoanalysis – over there, by Psychology and Religion.'

I looked. The only people who ever went near

Psychology and Religion were a man with a ponytail who wore a T-shirt, very dirty, that said EGO on one side and ID on the other, and a pair of women who pretended to be witches and were researching Wicca In Our Time. All three were over there, passing notes to one another as they weren't allowed to speak. Jung could wait.

'Who was Gertrude Stein?'

'A modernist. She wrote without regard to meaning.'

'Is that why she is under Humour, like Spike Milligan?'

'Within the Dewey decimal system there is a certain amount of discretion. That is another of its strengths. It saves us from confusion but it allows us freedom of thought. My predecessor will have felt that Gertrude Stein was too modern a modernist for English Literature A–Z, and in any case, although she wrote in English, or approximately so, she was an American and she lived in Paris. She is now dead.'

I took *The Autobiography of Alice B. Toklas* back to the Mini and I drove the Mini round to Mrs Ratlow's. I didn't go in for a while. I could hear her shouting at the boys.

I looked through the kitchen window of the neat little house – not a terrace like Water Street, but almost a cottage and backing onto fields. The huge hulking boys were eating their supper and Mrs Ratlow was ironing and reading Shakespeare from a music stand set up by the ironing board. She had taken off her polyester jacket and was in a Bri-Nylon blouse with short sleeves. Her arms were fat and dimpled. Her chest was wrinkled and slack and fleshy and red. She was everything Nabokov loathed.

Her eyes were bright reading Shakespeare, and every time she finished ironing one of the huge hulking shirts, she stopped, turned the page, hung the shirt, and got another from the pile.

She was wearing fluffy slippers, pink on the black-and-white lino.

She was giving me a chance. Winter was coming and it was cold sleeping in the Mini, and the condensation from a night's breathing meant that I woke up with drops of water all over me, like a leaf in the morning.

I had no idea whether any of what I was doing was the right thing to do. I talked to myself all the time, out loud, debating with myself my situation. I was lucky in one way because our church had always emphasised how important it is to concentrate on good things – blessings – not just bad things. And that is what I did at night when I curled up to sleep in my sleeping bag. There were very good things; there was Janey and there were my books. Leaving home meant that I could keep both without fear.

I got out my key, then I rang the bell out of politeness. One of the huge hulks opened the door. Mrs Ratlow came out. 'Help her with her things, you two, do I have to do it all?'

I had a tiny room that looked over the back fields. I put my books in piles and folded my clothes; three pairs of jeans, two pairs of shoes, four jumpers, four shirts and a week's supply of socks and knickers. And a duffel coat.

'Is that it?

'There's a tin-opener and some crockery and a

camping stove, and a towel and a sleeping bag but they can stay in the car.'

'You'll need a hot-water bottle.'

'I've got one, and a flashlight and shampoo.'

'All right then. Get some jam and bread and go to bed.'

She watched me as I got out Gertrude Stein.

'S,' she said.

Gertrude and Alice are living in Paris. They are helping the Red Cross during the war. They are driving along in a two-seater Ford shipped from the States. Gertrude likes driving but she refuses to reverse. She will only go forward because she says that the whole point of the twentieth century is progress.

The other thing that Gertrude won't do is read the map. Alice Toklas reads the map and Gertrude sometimes takes notice and sometimes not.

It is going dark. There are bombs exploding. Alice is losing patience. She throws down the map and shouts at Gertrude: 'THIS IS THE WRONG ROAD.'

Gertrude drives on. She says, 'Right or wrong, this is the road and we are on it.'

10

This Is The Road

IDECIDED TO APPLY TO read English at the
University of Oxford because it was the most
impossible thing I could do. I knew no one who had
been to university and although clever girls were
encouraged to go to teacher training college, or to
take their accountancy exams, Oxford and Cambridge
were not on the list of things to do before you die.

The Equal Pay Act had become law in Britain in
1970, but no woman I knew got anything like equal
pay – or believed that she should.

In the industrial north of England traditional kinds
of blue-collar employment were strong – factory work,
manufacture, mining, and men held the economic
power.

The women held together the family and the
community, but the invisibility of women's contribu-
tion, not measured or paid for, or socially rewarded,
meant that my world was full of strong able women
who were 'housewives' and had to defer to their men.
My mother did it to my father. She held him in
contempt (and that wasn't fair), but she called him
the head of the household (and that wasn't true). That
marital/domestic pattern was repeated everywhere I
looked.

Few women I knew had professional or managerial

jobs and those who did were unmarried. Most of my female teachers at school were unmarried. Mrs Ratlow was a widow, and she was head of English, but she still did all the cooking and cleaning for her two sons, and she never took holidays because she said – and I will never forget it: 'When a woman alone is no longer of any interest to the opposite sex, she is only visible where she has some purpose.'

It is quite a quote, and should have made her a feminist, but she had no time for feminism as a movement. She adored men, even though the lack of one rendered her invisible in her own eyes – the saddest place in the township of invisible places a woman can occupy. Germaine Greer had published *The Female Eunuch* in 1970 but none of us had read it.

We were not sophisticated. We were northerners. We didn't live in a big city like Manchester, and feminism seemed not to have reached us.

'Battleaxe' has always been a word used both for and against the strong northern working-class woman. That cleaver image split our identity too. Northern women were tough, and reckoned that way in the home and in popular comedy – all the seaside postcards were drawings of weedy little men and dominating women – and in the drunken working men's clubs, stage acts like Les Dawson dressed up in headscarves and aprons, parodying, but also celebrating, the formidable women the men loved, feared, and were dependent upon. Yet those women who were supposed to stand at the door waiting to whack their men with a rolling pin had no economic clout. And when they had, they hid it.

The women I knew who ran their own small

THIS IS THE ROAD

businesses, like the market stall I worked on, or the fish and chip shop that supplied me with many of my meals, pretended it was their husband's enterprise, and that they just worked there.

When we had our one and only sex education lesson at school it was not about sex at all, but sexual economics. We should pay our own way, because that was the modern thing to do, but we should give the boy the money beforehand, so that he could be seen to pay. We were only talking bus fares and cinema tickets, but later, when we managed the household budget, we should make sure he knew that everything was his. Male pride, I think the teacher called it. I thought it was the stupidest thing I had ever heard; a flat earth theory of social relations.

The only women who were contentedly living the life they wanted without pretending socially were the pair who ran the sweet shop, but they had to pretend sexually, and weren't able to be openly gay. People laughed at them, and one wore a balaclava.

I was a woman. I was a working-class woman. I was a woman who wanted to love women without guilt or ridicule. Those three things formed the basis of my politics, not the unions, or class war as understood by the male Left.

The Left has taken a long time to fully include women as independent and as equals – and no longer to enfold women's sexuality into a response to male desire. I felt uncomfortable and sidelined by what I knew of left-wing politics. And I wasn't looking to improve the conditions of my life. I wanted to change my life out of all recognition.

*

In the late 1970s, Margaret Thatcher appeared, talking about a new culture of risk and reward – one where you could achieve, one where you could be anything you wanted to be, if you would only work hard enough and be prepared to abandon the safety nets of tradition.

I had already left home. I was already working evenings and weekends to get through school. I had no safety net.

Thatcher seemed to me to have better answers than the middle-class men who spoke for the Labour Party, and the working-class men who campaigned for a 'family' wage, and wanted their women at home.

I had no respect for family life. I had no home. I had rage and courage. I was smart. I was emotionally disconnected. I didn't understand gender politics. I was the ideal prototype for the Reagan/Thatcher revolution.

I sat my Oxford entrance exam, coached by Mrs Ratlow, got an interview and bought a coach ticket to Oxford.

I had applied to St Catherine's because it had a new modern feel, because it was a mixed college, and because it had been formed out of the St Catherine's Society – a kind of sad satellite of the established Oxford colleges, founded for students too poor to attend Oxford proper.

But now it was Oxford proper. And maybe I could go there.

I got off the bus in Oxford and asked my way to St Catherine's. I felt like Jude the Obscure in Thomas Hardy's novel, and I was determined not to hang myself.

I had no idea that there could be such a beautiful city, or places like the colleges, with quadrangles and lawns, and that sense of energetic quiet that I still find so seductive.

I had been given overnight accommodation, and meals were provided in college, but I was too intimidated by the confidence of the other candidates to go in and eat with them.

I was unable to speak clearly during my interviews because for the first time in my life I felt that I looked wrong and sounded wrong. Everybody else seemed relaxed, though I am sure that was not true. They certainly had better clothes and different accents. I knew I was not being myself, but I didn't know how to be myself there. I hid the self that I was and had no persona to put in its place. A few weeks later I heard that I had not been given a place.

I was in despair. Mrs Ratlow said we must look at other options; to me, there were no other options. I was not interested in options; I was interested in Oxford.

So I came up with a plan.

I had passed my driving test at last, sold the Mini I didn't really own, and bought a road-legal Hillman Imp that cost me £40. The doors didn't work, but it had a good engine. As long you were prepared to wriggle in through the glass flap at the back, you could go quite a long way.

Janey said she would come with me, so we took my tent and set off to Oxford, travelling at 50 mph, the Imp's maximum speed, with frequent stops to add petrol, oil, water and brake fluid. We had two eggs with us in case the radiator leaked. In those days you could easily repair a radiator by dropping a broken egg into it, just as a fan belt could be replaced with a nylon stocking, and a snapped clutch cable with two bolts and a can of Tizer (holes in either end of can, bolts tied either end of snapped cable, bolts plus cable dropped into each end of can – you will find that with a bit of clunking, you can now depress the clutch).

Janey's family had a camp-site book and we looked up cheap camping at a golf club outside Oxford.

It took us about nine hours to get there but we had our bacon and beans and we were happy.

The next day I had an appointment to see the senior tutor and one of the English fellows – the other, fortunately for me, was away.

I had the usual problem of not being able to speak at all and then babbling like . . . Under stress I am a cross between Billy Budd and the Donkey in *Shrek*.

I spread my hands in despair and saw that the palms were covered in oil. The Imp had a leak.

So there was nothing for it but to explain at *Shrek*-speed about the Hillman Imp, and the tent, and the market stall where I worked, and a little bit about the Apocalypse and Mrs Winterson, and English Literature in Prose A – Z . . .

They already had a letter from Mrs Ratlow open on the desk. I don't know what she said, but Mrs Oliphant was mentioned.

'I want to be a better writer than her.'

'That shouldn't be too hard – though she did write a very good ghost story called –'

'*The Open Door*. I've read that. It's scary.'

For some reason Mrs Oliphant was on my side.

The senior tutor explained that St Catherine's was a progressive college, only founded in 1962, committed to bringing in pupils from state schools, and one of the few mixed colleges.

'Benazir Bhutto is here. Margaret Thatcher studied Chemistry at Somerville, you know.'

I didn't know and I didn't know who Benazir Bhutto was either.

'Would you like there to be a woman prime minister?'

Yes . . . In Accrington women couldn't be anything except wives or teachers or hairdressers or secretaries or do shop work. 'Well, they can be librarians, and I thought of doing that, but I want to write my own books.'

'What kind of books?'

'I don't know. I write all the time.'

'Most young people do.'

'Not in Accrington they don't.'

There was a pause. Then the English fellow asked me if I thought that women could be great writers. I was baffled by the question. It had never occurred to me.

'It's true they mostly come at the beginning of the alphabet – Austen, Brontës, Eliot . . .'

'We study those writers of course. Virginia Woolf is not on the syllabus though you will find her interesting – but compared to James Joyce . . .'

It was a reasonable introduction to the prejudices and pleasures of an Oxford degree course.

I left St Catherine's and walked down Holywell Street to Blackwell's bookshop. I had never seen a shop with five floors of books. I felt dizzy, like too much oxygen all at once. And I thought about women. All these books, and how long had it taken for women to be able to write their share, and why were there still so few women poets and novelists, and even fewer who were considered to be important?

I was so excited, so hopeful, and I was troubled too, by what had been said to me. As a woman would I be an onlooker and not a contributor? Could I study what I could never hope to achieve? Achieve it or not, I had to try.

And later, when I was successful, but accused of arrogance, I wanted to drag every journalist who misunderstood to this place, and make them see that for a woman, a working-class woman, to want to be a writer, to want to be a good writer, and to believe that you were good enough, that was not arrogance; that was politics.

Whatever happened that day worked out for me; I was given a place, deferred for a year.

And that took me straight to Margaret Thatcher and the 1979 election. Thatcher had the vigour and the arguments and she knew the price of a loaf of bread. She was a woman – and that made me feel that I too could succeed. If a grocer's daughter could be prime minister, then a girl like me could write a book that would be on the shelves of English Literature in Prose A–Z.

I voted for her.

It is commonplace now to say that Thatcher changed two political parties: her own, and the left-wing Labour opposition. It is less often remembered that Reagan in the US and Thatcher in the UK broke forever the post-war consensus – and that consensus had lasted for over thirty years.

Spin back to 1945, and whether you were on the Left or the Right in Britain or Western Europe, rebuilding societies after the war could not happen using the outdated and discredited neo-liberal economics of the free market – unregulated labour, unstable prices, no provision for the sick or the old or the unemployed. We were going to need housing, plenty of jobs, a welfare state, nationalisation of utilities and transport.

It was a real advance in human consciousness towards collective responsibility; an understanding that we owed something not only to our flag or to our country, to our children or our families, but to each other. Society. Civilisation. Culture.

That advance in consciousness did not come out of Victorian values or philanthropy, nor did it emerge from right-wing politics; it came out of the practical lessons of the war, and – *and this matters* – the superior arguments of socialism.

Britain's economic slow-down in the 1970s, our IMF bail-out, rocketing oil prices, Nixon's decision to float the dollar, unruly union disputes, and a kind of existential doubt on the Left, allowed the Reagan/ Thatcher 1980s Right to skittle away annoying arguments about a fair and equal society. We were going to follow Milton Friedman and his pals at the Chicago School of Economics back to the old free market laissez-faire, and dress it up as a new salvation.

Welcome TINA – There Is No Alternative.

In 1988, Thatcher's Chancellor of the Exchequer,

Nigel Lawson, called the post-war consensus, the 'post-war delusion'.

I did not realise that when money becomes the core value, then education drives towards utility or that the life of the mind will not be counted as a good unless it produces measurable results. That public services will no longer be important. That an alternative life to getting and spending will become very difficult as cheap housing disappears. That when communities are destroyed only misery and intolerance are left.

I did not know that Thatcherism would fund its economic miracle by selling off all our nationalised assets and industries.

I did not realise the consequences of privatising society.

I am driving under the viaduct and past the Factory Bottoms. As I drive past the Elim Pentecostal Church I see my dad coming out in his overalls. He's been painting. My foot lifts off the accelerator and I nearly stop. I want to say goodbye, but I don't because I can't. Did he see me? I don't know. I look in the mirror. He's going home. I am going away.

Out now, through Oswaldtwistle, past the dog-biscuit factory. There are some kids waiting by the side door for the broken bits of pink and green bone-shaped biscuits. Only one of them has a dog in tow.

I am in my Morris Minor van – successor to the Imp – loaded up with a bicycle and a trunk of books, a small suitcase of clothes and a pack of sardine sandwiches, and twenty gallons of petrol in tins because no one has told me that you can buy petrol on the motorway. As the dynamo on the Minor is faulty, I dare not switch off the engine, so I have to pull up on the hard shoulder of the motorway, run round and fill up with fuel, and set off again. I don't care.

I am going to Oxford.

11

Art and Lies

O N OUR FIRST EVENING AS undergraduates, our tutor turned to me and said, 'You are the working-class experiment.' Then he turned to the woman who was to become and remain my closest friend, and he said, 'You are the black experiment.'

We soon realised that our tutor was malevolently gay and that the five women in our year would receive no tuition. We were going to have to educate ourselves.

In a way it didn't matter. Books were everywhere and all we had to do was to read them – starting with *Beowulf* and ending with Beckett, and not worrying that there appeared to be only four women novelists – the Brontës, who came as a team, George Eliot, Jane Austen – and one woman poet, Christina Rossetti. She is not a great poet, unlike Emily Dickinson, but no one was going to tell us about great women. Oxford was not a conspiracy of silence as far as women were concerned; it was a conspiracy of ignorance. We formed our own reading group, and that soon included contemporary writers – women as well as men – and feminism. Suddenly I was reading Doris Lessing and Toni Morrison, Kate Millett and Adrienne Rich. They were like a new Bible.

142

But in spite of its sexism, snobbery, patriarchal attitudes and indifference to student welfare, the great thing about Oxford was its seriousness of purpose and the unquestioned belief that the life of the mind was at the heart of civilised life.

Although our tutor denigrated and undermined us, for no better reason than that we were women, we were tacitly upheld by the ethos of the university in our passion for reading, thinking, knowing, discussing.

That made a huge difference to me. It was like living in a library, and that was where I had always been happiest.

The more I read the more I fought against the assumption that literature is for the minority – of a particular education or class. Books were my birthright too. I will not forget my excitement at discovering that the earliest recorded poem in the English language was composed by a herdsman in Whitby around AD 680 ('Caedmon's Hymn') when St Hilda was the abbess of Whitby Abbey.

Imagine it . . . a woman in charge and an illiterate cowhand making a poem of such great beauty that educated monks wrote it down and told it to visitors and pilgrims.

It is a lovely story – Caedmon would rather be with the cows than with people, and he doesn't know any poetry or songs, and so at the end of the feasts in the abbey, when all are invited to sing or recite, Caedmon always rushes back to the cows where he can be on his own. But that night, an angel comes and tells him to sing – if he can sing to the cows, he can sing to the angel. Caedmon says sadly that he doesn't know any songs, but the angel tells him to sing one anyway – about the creation of the world. And Caedmon opens his mouth and there is the song. (Have a look at an early account of this in Bede: *History of the English Church and Peoples.*)

The more I read, the more I felt connected across time to other lives and deeper sympathies. I felt less isolated. I wasn't floating on my little raft in the present; there were bridges that led over to solid ground. Yes, the past is another country, but one that we can visit, and once there we can bring back the things we need.

Literature is common ground. It is ground not managed wholly by commercial interests, nor can it be strip-mined like popular culture – exploit the new thing then move on.

There's a lot of talk about the tame world versus the wild world. It is not only a wild nature that we need as human beings; it is the untamed open space of our imaginations.

Reading is where the wild things are.

At the end of my first term at Oxford we were reading T. S. Eliot's *Four Quartets*.

We move above the moving tree
In light upon the figured leaf
And hear upon the sodden floor
Below, the boarhound and the boar
Pursue their pattern as before
But reconciled among the stars.

I was thinking about the pattern; the past is so hard to shift. It comes with us like a chaperone, standing between us and the newness of the present – the new chance.

I was wondering if the past could be redeemed – could be 'reconciled' – if the old wars, the old enemies, the boarhound and the boar, might be able to find peace of a kind.

I was wondering this because I was thinking of visiting Mrs Winterson.

That there might be a level we can reach above the ordinary conflict is a seductive one. Jung argued that a conflict can never be resolved on the level at which it arises – at that level there is only a winner and a loser, not a reconciliation. The conflict must be got above – like seeing a storm from higher ground.

And there's a wonderful passage too, at the end of Chaucer's *Troilus and Criseyde*, where Troilus, defeated and dead, is taken up to the Seventh Sphere and he looks down on the sublunar world – ours – and laughs because he realises how absurd it all is – the things that mean so much, the feuds we carry, the irreconcilables.

The medieval mind loved the idea of mutability and everything happening chaotic and misunderstood under the sphere of the moon. When we look up at the sky and the stars we imagine we are looking out at the universe. The medieval mind imagined itself as looking *in* – that Earth was a seedy outpost, Mrs Winterson's cosmic dustbin – and that the centre was – well, at the centre – the nucleus of God's order proceeding from love.

I like it that order should proceed from love.

I understood, in a very dimly lit way, that I would need to find the place where my own life could be reconciled with itself. And I knew that had something to do with love.

I wrote to Mrs Winterson asking if she would like me to come back for the Christmas holidays – and could I bring a friend? Yes, she said, which was unusual.

She didn't ask what I had been doing since we had last seen each other – no mention of happy/normal, or leaving home, or going to Oxford. I didn't try to explain. Neither of us thought that was odd because in Winterson-world it wasn't odd.

There she was with her new electronic organ and her home-built CB radio and headphones the size of alien-life detection devices.

There I was with my friend Vicky Licorish. I had already warned Mrs W that she was black.

This was a great success to begin with because Mrs Winterson loved missionary work, and seemed to think that my having a best friend who was black was a kind of missionary endeavour all of its own. She went round to veterans of Africa and asked, 'What do they eat?'

The answer was pineapples. I don't know why. Are there any pineapples in Africa? In any case Vicky's family was from St Lucia.

Mrs Winterson was not a racist. Hers was a missionary kind of tolerance, and as such it was patronising, but she would not hear a slur against anyone on the grounds of colour or ethnicity.

That was unusual at a time when Pakistanis had

begun to arrive in noticeable numbers in white working-class towns where employment was already in short supply. Then, as now, nobody talked about the legacy of Empire. Britain had colonised, owned, occupied or interfered with half the world. We had carved up some countries and created others. When some of the world we had made by force wanted something in return, we were outraged.

But the Elim Church welcomed everyone and we were taught to make an effort for 'our friends from other shores'.

When Vicky and I arrived in Accrington, Mrs Winterson gave her a blanket she had knitted so that Vicky would not be cold. 'They feel the cold,' she told me.

Mrs Winterson was an obsessive and she had been knitting for Jesus for about a year. The Christmas tree had knitted decorations on it, and the dog was fastened inside a Christmas coat of red wool with white snowflakes. There was a knitted nativity and all the shepherds were wearing scarves because this was Bethlehem on the bus route to Accrington.

My dad opened the door wearing a new knitted waistcoat and matching knitted tie. The whole house had been reknitted.

Never mind. There was no sign of the revolver. Mrs W was wearing her best teeth.

'Vicky,' she said, 'sit down. I've made you cheese on toast with *pineapples*.'

Vicky assumed this was some Lancashire delicacy.

The next day there was gammon and pineapple followed by tinned pineapple chunks. Then there were pineapple fritters and pineapple upside-down cake and pineapples and cream and Chinese chicken and pineapple and pineapple and cubes of Cheddar on cocktail sticks stuck into half a cabbage wrapped in tinfoil.

Eventually Vicky said, 'I don't like pineapple.'

This was a terrible mistake. Mrs Winterson's mood changed at once. She announced that the next meal would be beefburgers. We said fine, but we were going out that night to eat scampi and chips in the pub.

About ten o'clock we returned to find Mrs Winterson standing grimly at the gas oven. There was a dreadful smell of burntness and oil and fat and meat.

In the little lean-to kitchen Mrs Winterson was mechanically flipping over some black things about the size of buttons.

'I've been cooking these beefburgers since six o'clock,' she said.

'But you knew we were going out.'

'You knew I was cooking beefburgers.'

We didn't know what to do so we went to bed – Vicky upstairs and me in the front room on a blow-up lilo. The next morning at breakfast the table was set. In the middle was a pyramid of unopened tins of pineapple and a Victorian postcard of two cats on their hind legs, dressed up as Mr and Mrs. The caption was: 'Nobody loves us.'

As we were wondering whether to run straight out to work or risk making toast, Mrs Winterson burst in, snatched up the postcard, and threw it back down on the table. 'That's your dad and me,' she said.

Vicky and I were working at the mental hospital

over Christmas; the vast Victorian pile where I had lived and worked during my year off. It was laid out in extensive grounds, with its own fire engine and social club. It was home to the deranged, the dangerous, the damaged and the damned. Some of the older residents had been locked up for having a baby, or trying to kill a baby, and some had been locked up with their babies. It was a strange world, both solitary and social.

I liked working there, cleaning the wards of vomit and shit and serving meals from giant tin trays. I worked twelve-hour shifts. Maybe the huge madness calmed my own disturbances. I felt compassion. And I felt lucky. It is easy to go mad.

The only thing I hated was the drugs trolley. Inmates were sedated and tranquillised – syringes and tablets look kinder than padded cells and straitjackets but I am not so sure. The wards smelled of Valium and Largactil – that's the one that rots your teeth.

Vicky and I went to and from our work there, trying not to notice that back home in Water Street the atmosphere was crazier than anything at work. The house was darkening and cracking – like something out of Poe. The Christmas decorations were up and the coloured lights were on but that just made it more frightening.

For about a week Mrs Winterson had not spoken to us. Then one night we got home, and it was snowing, and there were carol singers in the street. I realised it was the church meeting at our house.

Mrs Winterson was in gay mood. She had on a nice dress and when Vicky and I arrived she greeted us warmly. 'I'll bring round the dinner wagon – would you like a party pie?'

'What's a dinner wagon?' said Vicky, thinking of stagecoaches and shoot-outs.

'It's a hostess trolley for northerners,' I said, as Mrs Winterson careered into the parlour loaded with party pies on her heated element.

At that moment a rival group of carol singers arrived at the front door – probably the Salvation Army, but Mrs W was having none of it. She opened the front door and shouted, 'Jesus is here. Go away.'

'That was a bit harsh, Mum.'

'I have had a lot to put up with,' she said, looking meaningfully at me. 'I know the Bible tells us to turn the other cheek but there are only so many cheeks in a day.'

Vicky was struggling. Just before Christmas she went up to bed and found that her pillowcase had no pillow in it; it was stuffed with religious tracts about the Apocalypse. She was beginning to discover what it was like to live in End Time.

'It's hard for you where you come from,' said Mrs Winterson.

'I was born in Luton,' said Vicky.

But it *was* hard for her. It was hard for anyone. The paperchains hanging from the ceiling began to look like a madman's manacles.

My dad was spending most of his time in the shed in the backyard making an installation for the church. I suppose it was a kind of evangelical altarpiece. The pastor wanted something for the Sunday school that could decorate the church without looking like a Catholic graven image as forbidden in Exodus.

Dad enjoyed making clay-cast figures and painting them. He was on figure number six.

'What is it?' asked Vicky.

It was the Seven Saved Dwarves: Snow White wasn't there, presumably because she was too near the Catholic heresy of the Virgin Mary. The dwarves had little nameplates: Hopeful, Faithful, Cheerful, Godly, Worthy, Ready and Willing.

Dad was painting quietly. 'Your mother is upset,' he said.

We both knew what that meant.

In the kitchen Mrs Winterson was making custard. She was stirring the pan obsessively like someone mixing the dark waters of the deep. As we came past her from the backyard, she said, without looking up from the pan, 'Sin. That's what spoils everything.'

Vicky was unused to a conversational style that included bouts of silence lasting for days, and sudden doomful announcements from a train of thought we were all supposed to share but never could. I could tell that Vicky was finding things a strain, and I felt that Dad was trying to warn me. I checked the duster drawer. The revolver was not there.

'I think it's time for us to leave,' I said to Vicky.

The next morning I told Mum we were leaving. She said, 'You do it on purpose.'

The house. The two-up two-down. The long dark lobby and the poky rooms. The yard with the outside loo and the coal-hole, the dustbins and the dog kennel.

'Goodbye, Mum.'

She didn't answer. Not then. Not later. I never went back. I never saw her again.

Intermission

IN MY WORK I HAVE pushed against the weight of clock time, of calendar time, of linear unravellings. Time may be what stops everything happening at once, but time's domain is the outer world. In our inner world, we can experience events that happened to us in time as happening simultaneously. Our non-linear self is uninterested in 'when', much more interested in 'wherefore'.

I am more than halfway through my biological life and about halfway through my creative life. I measure time as we all do, and partly by the fading body, but in order to challenge linear time, I try and live in total time. I recognise that life has an inside as well as an outside and that events separated by years lie side by side imaginatively and emotionally.

Creative work bridges time because the energy of art is not time-bound. If it were we should have no interest in the art of the past, except as history or documentary. But our interest in art is our interest in ourselves both now and always. Here and forever. There is a sense of the human spirit as always existing. This makes our own death bearable. Life + art is a boisterous communion/communication with the dead. It is a boxing match with time.

I like the line in T. S. Eliot's *Four Quartets* – '*that which is only living/Can only die*'. That's time's arrow, the flight from womb to tomb. But life is more than an arrow.

The womb to tomb of an interesting life – but I can't write my own; never could. Not *Oranges*. Not now. I would rather go on reading myself as a fiction than as a fact.

The fact is that I am going to miss out twenty-five years. Maybe later . . .

12

The Night Sea Voyage

W HEN I WAS LITTLE – THE size that hides under
tables and climbs into drawers – I climbed into
a drawer believing that the drawer was a ship and the
rug a sea.

I found my message in a bottle. I found a birth
certificate. On the certificate were the names of my
birth parents.

I never told anyone about this.

I never wanted to find my birth parents – if one
set of parents felt like a misfortune, two sets would
be self-destructive. I had no understanding of family
life. I had no idea that you could like your parents,
or that they could love you enough to let you be
yourself.

I was a loner. I was self-invented. I didn't believe
in biology or biography. I believed in myself. Parents?
What for? Except to hurt you.

But when I was thirty and I wrote the TV scripts
for *Oranges Are Not the Only Fruit*, I called the main
character Jess. She is Jeanette in the book, but TV is
so literal, and it was hard enough to fight for ambi-
guity and playfulness *and* use your own name, even
when the thing was filed under Literature. File it
under TV drama and I thought I would find myself
tied to a 'true' story forever.

That happened anyway . . . but I tried.

155

So I had to choose a name, and I chose the name on the birth certificate I had found. It seemed that my mother's name was Jessica, so I would call my character Jess.

Oranges won everything – BAFTAs, RTS awards, a script award for me at Cannes, numerous foreign prizes – and it was a big talking point in 1990, because of the content, and because of the way we handled the content. It was a landmark for gay culture, and I hope it was a cultural landmark too. I think it was. A 2008 poll of Best Ever BBC Dramas put *Oranges* at number 8.

I reckoned with all the fuss, including and especially in the tabloid press (end of decency as we know it, etc.), that my mother Jess would hear about it, and put two and two together.

No.

Flash forward to 2007 and I have done nothing about finding my past. It isn't 'my past', is it? I have written over it. I have recorded on top of it. I have repainted it. Life is layers, fluid, unfixed, fragments. I never could write a story with a beginning, a middle and an end in the usual way because it felt untrue to me. That is why I write as I do and how I write as I do. It isn't a method; it's me.

I was writing a novel called *The Stone Gods*. It is set in the future, though the second section is set in the past. It imagines our world in its protean state being discovered by an advanced but destructive civilisation whose own planet is dying. A mission is sent to Planet Blue. The mission does not return.

Whenever I write a book, one sentence forms in

my mind, like a sandbar above the waterline. They are like the texts written up on the walls when we all lived at 200 Water Street; exhortations, maxims, lighthouse signals flashed out as memory and warning.

The Passion: 'I'm telling you stories. Trust me.'

Written on the Body: 'Why is the measure of love loss?'

The PowerBook: 'To avoid discovery I stay on the run. To discover things for myself, I stay on the run.'

Weight: 'The free man never thinks of escape.'

The Stone Gods: 'Everything is imprinted forever with what it once was.'

In my previous novel, *Lighthousekeeping*, I had been working with the idea of a fossil record. Now I was there again – the sense of something written over, yes, but still distinct. The colours and forms revealed under ultraviolet light. The ghost in the machine that breaks through into the new recording.

What was the 'imprint'?

I was having a hard time. My six-year relationship with director Deborah Warner was rocky and unhappy for us both.

I was trying to write. The book was pushing me. Creative work is a lie detector. I wanted to lie to myself – if lies are the comforts and the cover-ups.

In the spring of 2007, my father's second wife Lillian died unexpectedly. She was ten years younger than him, and had been lively and merry. A botched hip replacement had led to foot gangrene, foot gangrene had led to no walking, no walking had led to diabetes, diabetes had led to hospital for a three-day stay. Three weeks later she left the hospital in a coffin.

Dad and Lillian had both taken respites in a care home in Accrington run by a wonderful woman called Nesta. She had worked as a comedienne on a cruise ship – and you need a sense of humour to run a care home. She had finally stopped telling jokes for a living and taken over the family care home business. She and I talked about things, and decided Dad should go and live there when there was a vacancy. He would get to church on Sundays and be taken out midweek and there would be plenty of people to visit him. I would make the 350-mile round trip to see him once a month.

I drove up to Accrington and cleared out his bungalow and was busy arranging everything in the preoccupied way that you do – the interminable paperwork of death.

All the photos had definitely gone, taken by the ghastly Uncle Alec (him of the Dobermanns), for what purpose I don't know. There was nothing really of the old days, but there was a locked chest.

Treasure? I have always believed that the buried treasure is really there . . .

I went to my car, got a screwdriver and a hammer, and drove the screwdriver into the mouth of the padlock. It sprang open.

To my horror the chest was full of Royal Albert, including a three-tier cake stand. Why had Dad hidden the remnants of the Royal Albert in a Long John Silver pirate chest?

There were some other bits of crockery that brought the taste of my childhood back into my mouth. Mrs Winterson's 'cottage' plates, hand-painted with golden edges, and in the centre a little cottage on its own in a wood . . . (rather like where I live now).

There were Dad's medals from the war and some notes and letters from Mrs W, and some sad personal items, and some horrible things about me, so I threw those away, and a few of her weekly shopping lists and budgets, and saddest of all, her letter to Dad, written in very shaky copperplate handwriting, telling him step by step what to do after she was dead – the insurance policy for the funeral . . . the pension papers . . . the deeds for the house.

Poor Dad – did he ever expect to outlive two wives? Unlike Mrs Winterson, Lillian had left no instructions – but this time it was all right because this time I could be there.

I lifted out the Royal Albert salmon platter. Underneath was a little box. A box hiding in a box . . . Not locked . . . a bit of jewellery, a few envelopes, a few papers carefully folded.

The first bit of paper was a court order dated 1960. It was my formal adoption paper. The second bit of paper was a kind of MOT of Baby: I was not a mental defective. I was well enough to be adopted. I had been breastfed . . .

And I had had a name – violently crossed out. The top of the paper had been torn too, so that I could not read the name of the doctor or the organisation, and the names at the bottom had been ripped away.

I looked at the court order. That too had a name – my other name – crossed out.

Typewriters and yellow paper. So old. Those things look like a hundred years ago. I am a hundred years ago. Time is a gap.

★

It is dark now. I am sitting in my coat on the floor of the empty bungalow. I feel emptied of the familiar furniture. I have opened a door into a room with furniture I don't recognise. There is a past after all, no matter how much I have written over it.

Like the name on the pieces of the paper – the name written over – my past is there – here – and it is now. The gap has closed around me. I feel trapped.

I don't know why this matters. Why this feels so bad. Why did they never tell me or show me? Why would they? And a baby is a baby. The baby begins again. No biography, no biology.

Then a string of lines starts replaying in my head – lines from my own books – 'I keep writing this so that one day she will read it.' 'Looking for you, looking for me, I guess I've been looking for us both all my life . . .'

I have written love narratives and loss narratives – stories of longing and belonging. It all seems so obvious now – the Wintersonic obsessions of love, loss and longing. It is my mother. It is my mother. It is my mother.

But mother is our first love affair. Her arms. Her eyes. Her breast. Her body.

And if we hate her later, we take that rage with us into other lovers. And if we lose her, where do we find her again?

I tend to work obsessively with texts, and I embed them in my work. The Grail legend is there – one glimpse and the most precious thing in the world is gone forever, and then the quest is to find it again.

The Winter's Tale. My favourite Shakespeare play: an

abandoned baby. A sick world which shall not be righted again if 'that which is lost be not found'.

Read that line. Not 'that which was lost' or 'has been lost'. Instead, 'is lost'. The grammar shows us how serious is the loss. Something that happened a long time ago, yes – but not the past. This is the old present, the old loss still wounding each day.

Soon after that time I began to go mad. There is no other way to put it.

Deborah left me. We had a final fearful row, triggered by my insecurities and Deborah's detachment, and the next day we were over. The End.

Deborah was right to go. What had begun with great hope had become slow torture. I do not blame her for anything. Much about us together was marvellous. But as I was to discover, I have big problems around home, making homes, making homes with someone. Deborah loves being away from home and thrives on it. She is a cuckoo.

I love coming home – and my idea of happiness is to come home to someone I love. We were not able to resolve that difference and what I didn't know was how something as straightforward as a difference could lead to something as complex as a breakdown. The sudden unexpected abandonment, constellated as it was around the idea of/impossibility of home, lit a fuse that spat and burned its way towards a walled-up opening a long way back inside me. Inside that walled-up opening, smothered in time like an anchorite, was my mother.

Deborah did not intend to detonate the 'lost loss', and I didn't even know it was there – not in any matter of fact way of knowing – though my behaviour patterns were a clue.

My agony over calling Deborah and finding that she would never return my calls, my bewilderment and rage, these emotional states were taking me nearer to the sealed door where I had never wanted to go.

That makes it sound like a conscious choice. The psyche is much smarter than consciousness allows. We bury things so deep we no longer remember there was anything to bury. Our bodies remember. Our neurotic states remember. But we don't.

I started waking up at night and finding myself on all fours shouting 'Mummy, Mummy'. I was wet with sweat.

Trains arrived. Train doors opened. I could not board. Humiliated, I cancelled events, arrangements, never able to say why. Sometimes I didn't go out for days, get dressed for days, sometimes I wandered around the big garden in my pyjamas, sometimes I ate, sometimes not at all, or you could see me on the grass with a tin of cold baked beans. The familiar sights of misery.

If I had lived in London, or any city, I would have killed myself by being careless in traffic – my car, someone else's car. I was thinking about suicide because it had to be an option. I had to be able to think about it and on good days I did so because it gave me back a sense of control – for one last time I would be in control.

On bad days I just held onto the thinning rope.

The rope was poetry. All that poetry I learned

when I had to keep my library inside me now offered a rescue rope.

There is a field in front of my house, high up, sheltered by a drystone wall and opened by a long view of hills. When I could not cope I went and sat in that field against that wall and fixed on that view.

The countryside, the natural world, my cats, and English Literature A–Z were what I could lean on and hold onto.

My friends never failed me and when I could talk I did talk to them.

But often I could not talk. Language left me. I was in the place before I had any language. The abandoned place.

Where are you?

But what is really your own never does leave you. I could not find words, not directly, for my own state, but every so often I could write, and I did so in lit-up explosions, that for a time showed me that there was still a world – proper and splendid. I could be my own flare to see by. Then the light went out again.

I had already written two books for children: *The King of Capri*, a picture book, and a novel for older children called *Tanglewreck*. *Tanglewreck* imagines a world where time, like oil or water or any other commodity, is running out.

I wrote these books for my godchildren, the children and the books giving me uncomplicated delight.

Arriving back from Holland in December 2007 I had used up all my resources giving an important public lecture and trying to act normal. I was sweating again, and when I got into the house I couldn't even manage to light the fire. So I sat in my overcoat with a tin of baked beans in my hands, and both cats on my knees.

I thought of a story – a Christmas story, the Christmas story from the donkey's point of view called 'The Lion, the Unicorn and Me'. The donkey gets a golden nose when he lifts up his head to bray and the angel's foot, dangling from the wormy rafters of the stable, brushes his nose.

I was the donkey. I needed a golden nose.

I wrote the story that night – until about five in the morning, then slept and slept, for nearly twenty-four hours.

The story was published in *The Times*. On Christmas Eve, a very nice lady sent me an email saying it had made her cry and it had made her little girl laugh and cry, and could her publishing house illustrate it and publish it?

That is what happened.

And it wasn't the end of the books rescuing me. If poetry was a rope, then the books themselves were rafts. At my most precarious I balanced on a book, and the books rafted me over the tides of feelings that left me soaked and shattered.

Feeling. I didn't want to feel.

The best reprieve for me at that time was to go to Paris and hide in the bookshop Shakespeare and Company.

I had become friends with the owner, Sylvia Whitman, a young woman whose enormous energy and enthusiasm carry her through most things. Her father George, who opened the shop on its present site by Notre-Dame in 1951, still lives upstairs, perched like an old eagle.

Sylvia arranged for me to stay in the unmodernised old-fashioned Hotel Esmeralda next door to the shop. On the top floor, with no phone, no TV, just a bed and a desk, and a view of the church, I found I could sleep and even work.

I could sit in the antiquarian part of the bookshop all day and much of the night, reading with Sylvia's dog beside me, and when I needed to walk, the dog, Colette, came too. It was a simple, safe escape.

At the shop I had no responsibilities and I was looked after. Arriving once with a chest infection, Sylvia wouldn't let me go home. Instead she made me soup, changed my tickets, bought me pyjamas and kept me in bed.

There was a feel of the old days in the Accrington Public Library. I was safe. I was surrounded by books. My breathing became deeper and steadier and I was no longer haunted. Those times were temporary but they were precious.

I wasn't getting better. I was getting worse.

I did not go to the doctor because I didn't want pills. If this was going to kill me then let me be killed by it. If this was the rest of my life I could not live.

I knew clearly that I could not rebuild my life or put it back together in any way. I had no idea what might lie on the other side of this place. I only knew that the before-world was gone forever.

I had a sense of myself as a haunted house. I never knew when the invisible thing would strike – and it was like a blow, a kind of winding in the chest or stomach. When I felt it I would cry out at the force of it.

Sometimes I lay curled up on the floor. Sometimes I kneeled and gripped a piece of furniture.

This is one moment . . . know that another . . .

Hold on, hold on, hold on.

I love the natural world and I never ceased to see it. The beauty of trees and fields, of hills and streams, of the changing colours, of the small creatures so busy and occupied. My long hours walking or sitting in the field with my back against the wall, watching the clouds and the weather, allowed me some steadiness. It was because I knew all this would be there when I was not that I thought I could go. The world was beautiful. I was a speck in it.

There was a dead fox on the path I took. Not a mark on his strong red body. I moved him into the bushes. That would be enough for me too.

And I felt that I had done some good work. I had not wasted my life. I could go.

I wrote letters to my friends and to the children. I remember thinking that I wouldn't have to complete the end-of-year tax and VAT return. And I thought, 'I wonder if they fine you if you don't die of natural causes. Will Her Majesty's Revenue & Customs argue that I chose not to fill in my forms because I chose to kill myself? There is bound to be a penalty for that.'

So I was calm for a while and it seemed as if I had deferred the reckoning by looking it in the face.

Until the 1950s half the suicides in England were gassings. Household gas came from coal gas in those days and coal gas is high in carbon monoxide. Carbon monoxide is colourless and odourless and the enemy of oxygen-dependent creatures. It causes hallucinations and depression. It can make you see apparitions – indeed, there is an argument that the haunted house is the house whose vapours are not spectral but chemical. This may well be true. The nineteenth century was the century of frightful spectres and shadowy visitations. It was the century of the supernatural in fiction and in the popular imagination.

Dracula, The Woman in White, The Turn of the Screw, Dr Jekyll and Mr Hyde, the visions of M. R. James and Edgar Allan Poe. The rise of the weekly seance.

The century of gas lamps and ghosts. They may have been the same thing. The classic image of a man or woman sitting up late by gaslight and seeing a ghost could have been a case of mild delirium caused by carbon-monoxide poisoning.

When natural gas was introduced in the 1960s, the British suicide rate fell by one-third – so perhaps that's why there have been fewer ghosts for us to see, or perhaps we are not hallucinating at home any more.

It is no longer easy to gas yourself. The oven won't do it and modern cars have catalytic converters fitted.

I had an old Porsche 911.

Herman Hesse called suicide a state of mind – and there are a great many people, nominally alive, who have committed a suicide much worse than physical death. They have vacated life.

I did not want to vacate life. I loved life. I love life. Life is too precious to me not to live it fully. I thought, 'If I cannot live then I must die.'

My time was up. That was the strongest feeling I had. The person who had left home at sixteen and blasted through all the walls in her way, and been fearless, and not looked back, and who was well known as a writer, controversially so (she's brilliant, she's rubbish), and who had made money, made her way, been a good friend, a volatile and difficult lover, who had had a couple of minor breakdowns and a psychotic period, but always been able to pull it back, to get on and go forward; that Jeanette Winterson person was done.

In February 2008 I tried to end my life. My cat was in the garage with me. I did not know that when I sealed the doors and turned on the engine. My cat was scratching my face, scratching my face, scratching my face.

Later that night, lying on the gravel and looking up at the stars – the miraculous stars and the wood that deepens the dark – I could hear a voice. I know I was having an hallucination but it was the hallucination I needed to have.

'Ye must be born again.' 'Ye must be born again' (John 3:7).

I had been twice born already, hadn't I – my lost mother and my new mother, Mrs Winterson – that double identity, itself a kind of schizophrenia – my sense of myself as being a girl who's a boy who's a boy who's a girl. A doubleness at the heart of things.

But then I understood something. I understood twice born was not just about being alive, but about choosing life. Choosing to be alive and consciously committing to life, in all its exuberant chaos – and its pain.

I had been given life and I had done my best with what I had been given. But there was no more to do there. Whatever had erupted through the coincidence/ synchronicity of finding those adoption papers and Deborah leaving me was my one and only chance at another chance.

It was a rope slung across space. It was a chance as near to killing me as to saving me and I believe it was an even bet which way it went. It was the loss of everything through the fierce and unseen return of the lost loss. The door into the dark room had swung open. The door at the bottom of the steps in our nightmares. The Bluebeard door with the bloodstained key.

The door had swung open. I had gone in. The room had no floor. I had fallen and fallen and fallen.

But I was alive.

And that night the cold stars made a constellation from the pieces of my broken mind.

There was no straight-line connection. You can tell that reading this. I want to show how it is when the mind works with its own brokenness.

In March 2008 I was in bed recovering and reading Mark Doty – *Dog Years*.

It is a memoir about living with dogs – actually it is a story about living with life. Living with life is very hard. Mostly we do our best to stifle life – to be tame or to be wanton. To be tranquillised or raging. Extremes have the same effect; they insulate us from the intensity of life.

And extremes – whether of dullness or fury – successfully prevent feeling. I know our feelings can be so unbearable that we employ ingenious strategies – unconscious strategies – to keep those feelings away. We do a feelings-swap, where we avoid feeling sad or lonely or afraid or inadequate, and feel angry instead. It can work the other way, too – sometimes you do need to feel angry, not inadequate; sometimes you do need to feel love and acceptance, and not the tragic drama of your life.

It takes courage to feel the feeling – and not trade it on the feelings-exchange, or even transfer it altogether to another person. You know how in couples one person is always doing the weeping or the raging while the other one seems so calm and reasonable?

I understood that feelings were difficult for me although I was overwhelmed by them.

I often hear voices. I realise that drops me in the crazy category but I don't much care. If you believe, as I do, that the mind wants to heal itself, and that the psyche seeks coherence not disintegration, then it isn't hard to conclude that the mind will manifest whatever is necessary to work on the job.

We now assume that people who hear voices do terrible things; murderers and psychopaths hear voices, and so do religious fanatics and suicide bombers. But in the past, voices were respectable – desired. The visionary and the prophet, the shaman and the wise-woman. And the poet, obviously. Hearing voices can be a good thing.

Going mad is the beginning of a process. It is not supposed to be the end result.

Ronnie Laing, the doctor and psychotherapist who became the trendy 1960s and 70s guru making madness fashionable, understood madness as a process that might lead somewhere. Mostly, though, it is so terrifying for the person inside it, as well as the people outside it, that the only route is drugs or a clinic.

And our madness-measure is always changing. Probably we are less tolerant of madness now than at any period in history. There is no place for it. Crucially, there is no time for it.

Going mad takes time. Getting sane takes time.

There was a person in me — a piece of me — however you want to describe it — so damaged that she was prepared to see me dead to find peace.

That part of me, living alone, hidden, in a filthy abandoned lair, had always been able to stage a raid on the rest of the territory. My violent rages, my destructive behaviour, my own need to destroy love and trust, just as love and trust had been destroyed for me. My sexual recklessness — not liberation. The fact that I did not value myself. I was always ready to jump off the roof of my own life. Didn't that have a romance to it? Wasn't that the creative spirit unbounded?

No.

Creativity is on the side of health — it isn't the thing that drives us mad; it is the capacity in us that tries to save us from madness.

The lost furious vicious child living alone in the bottom bog wasn't the creative Jeanette — she was the war casualty. She was the sacrifice. She hated me. She hated life.

There are so many fairy stories – you know them – where the hero in a hopeless situation makes a deal with a sinister creature and obtains what is needed – and it is needed – to go on with the journey. Later, when the princess is won, the dragon defeated, the treasure stored, the castle decorated, out comes the sinister creature and makes off with the new baby, or turns it into a cat, or – like the thirteenth fairy nobody invited to the party – offers a poisonous gift that kills happiness.

This misshapen murderous creature with its super-natural strength needs to be invited home – but on the right terms.

Remember the princess who kisses the frog – and yippee, there's a prince? Well, it is necessary to embrace the slimy loathsome thing usually found in the well or in the pond, eating slugs. But making the ugly hurt part human again is not an exercise for the well-meaning social worker in us.

This is the most dangerous work you can do. It is like bomb disposal but you are the bomb. That's the problem – the awful thing is you. It may be split off and living malevolently at the bottom of the garden, but it is sharing your blood and eating your food. Mess this up, and you will go down with the creature.

And – just to say – the creature loves a suicide. Death is part of the remit.

I am talking like this because what became clear to me in my madness was that I had to start talking – to the creature.

I was lying in bed reading *Dog Years*, and a voice outside of my head – not in it – said, 'Get up and start work.'

I got dressed immediately. I went over to my studio.

I lit the wood-burning stove, sat down with my coat on because the place was freezing, and wrote — *It began as all important things begin — by chance.*

From then on, every day, I wrote a book for children called *The Battle of the Sun.*

Every day I went to work, without a plan, without a plot, to see what I had to say.

And that is why I am sure that creativity is on the side of health. I was going to get better, and getting better began with the chance of the book.

It is not a surprise that it was a children's book. The demented creature in me was a lost child. She was willing to be told a story. The grown-up me had to tell it to her.

And one of the first things that invented itself in the new book was something called the Creature Sawn in Two.

The Creature who came into the room was cleaved in half straight down the middle, so that one half of him had one eye and one eyebrow, one nostril, one ear, one arm, one leg, one foot, and the other half had just the same

Well, nearly just the same, because as if the Creature did not astonish enough, one half of him was male and the other half of him was female. The female half had a bosom, or certainly half a bosom.

The Creature appeared to be made of flesh, like a human being, but what human being born is cleaved in half?

The Creature's clothes were as odd as the Creature itself. The male half wore a shirt with

173

one sleeve, and a pair of breeches with one leg, and where the other sleeve and other leg should have been was a cut-off and sewn-up side. The Creature had a sleeveless leather jerkin over his shirt, and his jerkin had not been altered in any way, so it looked as though half of it was unfilled with body, which was true.

Beneath the breeches, or perhaps the breech, as the garment must be called, having one leg and not two, was a stocking fastened at the knee, and a stout leather shoe on the bottom of the stocking.

The Creature had no beard, but wore in his single ear a single gold earring.

His other half was just as bizarre. This lady wore half a skirt, half a chemise and half a hat on her half of their head.

At her waist, or that portion of herself which would have been a waist, dangled a great bunch of keys. She wore no earrings but her hand, more slender than the other, had a ring on each finger.

The expression on either half of the face was disagreeable.

My own vicious disagreeable creature liked me writing *The Battle of the Sun*. She and I started talking. She said, 'No wonder Deb left you – why would she want to be with you? Even your own mother gave you away. You are worthless. I am the only one who knows it but you are worthless.'

I wrote this in my notebook. I decided that I was only prepared to talk to this savage lunatic for an hour a day – and while we were walking. She never wanted to go for a walk, but I made her.

Her conversational style was recriminatory (blame, fault, accusation, demands, guilt). She was part Mrs Winterson, part Caliban. Her preferred responses were non sequiturs. If I said, 'I want to talk about the coal-hole,' she said, 'You'd sleep with anybody, wouldn't you?' If I said, 'Why were we so hopeless at school?' she said, 'I blame nylon knickers.'

Our conversations were like two people using phrasebooks to say things neither understands; you think you asked the way to the church, but it translates as 'I need a safety pin for my hamster'.

It was mad – I said it was mad – but I was determined to go on with it. What made it possible was the sanity of the book in the mornings and the steadiness of gardening in the spring and summer evenings. Planting cabbages and beans is good for you. Creative work is good for you.

The afternoon madness session contained the oozing lunacy that had been everywhere. I noticed that I was no longer side-swiped and haunted. I was no longer being attacked by sweating terrors and unnamed fears.

Why didn't I take myself and the creature to therapy? I did, but it didn't work. The sessions felt false. I couldn't tell the truth, and anyway, she wouldn't come with me.

'Get in the car . . .' NO. 'Get in the car . . .' NO.

It was worse than having a toddler. She was a toddler, except that she was other ages too, because time doesn't operate on the inside as it does on the outside. She was sometimes a baby. Sometimes she was seven, sometimes eleven, sometimes fifteen.

Whatever she was, she wasn't going to therapy. 'It's a wank, it's a wank, it's a wank!'

I slammed the door. 'Do you want to learn to eat with a knife and fork?'

I don't know why I said that. She was feral.

So I went to therapy and she didn't. Pointless.

It wasn't all pointless though, because after therapy, in Oxford, I was always so fed up that I went to Blackwell's bookshop, and down to the Norrington Room, looking at the psychoanalysis shelves. The Norrington Room is a serious place – designed for the university, and stocking every text on brain/mind/psyche/self.

I had been reading Jung since 1995 – I bought the whole hardback set. I already had the whole hardback set of Freud, and I had always read Mind Body Spirit stuff, because if you are raised on the Bible, you don't just walk away, whatever anybody says.

Now, I was looking for something, and I found Neville Symington, a priest turned shrink, who had a simple direct style and was not afraid of talking about the spirit and the soul – not as religious experiences but as human experiences – that we are more than body and mind – and I think we are.

Symington helped, because I was getting well enough to want a framework in which to think about what was happening to me. Previously I had been holding on to the side of the open boat that was my life, and hoping not to drown under the next wave.

Occasionally the creature appeared when I was reading, to mock me, to hurt me, but now I could ask her to leave until our meeting the following day and, miraculously, she did.

It was summer. *The Battle of the Sun* was nearly finished. I was lonely and alone, but I was calm, and I was saner than I have ever been, insomuch as I knew there was a part of me that was in madness.

Symington talks about how the mad part will try to wreck the mind. That had been my experience. Now I could contain it.

A few months later we were having our afternoon walk when I said something about how nobody had cuddled us when we were little. I said 'us', not 'you'. She held my hand. She had never done that before; mainly she walked behind shooting her sentences.

We both sat down and cried.

I said, 'We will learn how to love.'

13

This Appointment Takes
Place In The Past

Dear Madam

With reference to your request regarding the above numbered file.

The District Judge has considered your application and made the following directions:

1. The copy birth certificate is not a copy of the entry in the Adopted Children Register.

2. Part 8B of the Practice Direction Section 1.3 requires the Application and Evidence of Identity 'must be taken to the Court', the Court makes a note on the application form. The original evidence of identity must be produced (not a copy).

3. After that a redacted copy of the relevant documents, specified in the practice direction, can be forwarded. The file is not open to inspection as a whole and cannot be sent to the Home Office.

Unfortunately it will therefore be necessary for you to attend personally at the Court and produce original evidence of identity together with a certified copy of the entry in the Register of Adopted Children which relates to you.

It was one of many exchanges with the court holding my adoption file.

I am an intelligent woman with plenty of resources but the adoption process skittled me. I did not know what was meant by 'the entry in the Register of Adopted Children' – and it took four emails to find out. I did know what 'redacted' meant, but I wondered if other people did (can't you just say 'the edited version'?), and I wondered what such a cold and formal letter does to people in the heated and upsetting process of looking for your other life.

As far as the court is concerned, adoption records are nothing more than an archive with legal implications, and are attended to in the dead and distant language of the law, obeying protocol that is difficult to follow. That isn't a good reason to engage a lawyer; it is a good reason to make the process simpler and less insensitive.

I wanted to stop. I wasn't so sure I had wanted to start.

I was lucky though, because I had fallen in love with Susie Orbach. We were quite new but she wanted me to feel that I was in a safe place with somebody who would give me support and, very simply, be there for me. 'We are together,' she said. 'That means you've got rights.' She laughed her big bold laugh.

I met Susie some time after I failed to interview her for her book *Bodies* – about the impact of advertising and pornography on women's bodies and self-image.

My father had died, and all work had to be put

aside. Eventually I wrote to Susie, just to say how much I had enjoyed her book – all her books. I had read *Fat Is A Feminist Issue* when I was nineteen. I had been rereading her *Impossibility of Sex*, and thinking I would try and write an answer to it – in the broadest sense – called *The Possibility of Love*.

I am always wondering about love.

Susie invited me to supper. She had been parted from her husband for about two years, after a thirty-four-year marriage. I had been by myself since Deborah and the breakdown. I was beginning to like being by myself again. But the big things in life are never planned. We had a very good evening; food, conversation, the sun setting behind her beech tree. I thought, 'She looks sad.' I wonder if I did too?

Over the next few weeks we wooed each other in fonts and pixels – an email courtship that couldn't be happening, I thought, because Susie was heterosexual and I have given up missionary work with heterosexual women. But something was going on and I had no idea what to do about it.

I had lunch with my friend, the writer Ali Smith. She said, 'Just kiss her.'

Susie went to talk to her daughter in New York. Lianna said, 'Just kiss her, Mummy.'

So we did.

In the place of trust with her I felt I could keep going with my search. Adoption begins on your own – you are solitary. The baby knows it has been abandoned – I am sure of that. Therefore, the journey back should not be done alone. The terrors and fears are

unexpected and out of control. You need someone to hold on to. Someone who will hold on to you. That's what Susie did for me day by day. Others of my friends did their part. Whatever else, the crazy time, and the adoption search, taught me to ask for help; not to act like Wonder Woman.

I had confided my fears to my friend Ruth Rendell. Ruth has known me since I was twenty-six, and she lent me a cottage to write in when I was trying to make my way. I wrote *The Passion* in her house. She had been the Good Mother – never judging, quietly supporting, letting me talk, letting me be.

She is a Labour peer, and therefore a member of the House of Lords. She knows a lot of people and she thought she could help. She summoned a few baronessess for a private discussion, and the consensus was that I should proceed with the utmost caution.

I am well known in the UK and if I was going to meet my mother I wanted her to meet me, not my public profile. And I could not face the newspapers getting hold of the story. *Oranges* is an adoption story, and *Oranges* is the book that is identified with me.

I may be paranoid but it is justified paranoia. I have had journalists stationed in my garden to 'discover' my girlfriends, and I fretted that some journalists would be only too happy to 'discover' lost mothers too.

So I just didn't feel comfortable filling in a form and putting it in the post and going and telling my story to a social worker – a mandatory requirement in the UK, if you want to open a closed adoption file.

My search was complicated by the fact that prior to 1976, all UK adoptions were made on the basis of closed records. Mothers and children alike were assured of lifetime anonymity. When the law changed, people like me could apply for our original birth certificates, and perhaps then contact our long-lost relatives. But everything has to be done visibly and formally. This seemed fraught to me.

Ruth put me in touch with Anthony Douglas, chief of Cafcass – the UK children and family court advisory service. He is adopted himself, and after a meeting where he understood my predicament, he offered to help me to trace my mother without the risk of the whole thing leaking into the public domain before I was ready.

I gave Anthony the names I had carried with me for forty-two years – the names of my parents – Jessica and John – and their surnames, but I can't write those here.

A few weeks later he called me to say that my file had been found – but only just, because the Southport Records Office – in my case the basement – had been flooded with seawater and many files had been irretrievably damaged. I looked up to heaven. Mrs Winterson had obviously heard that I was hunting and arranged a flood.

A week later Anthony called again – my file had been opened but the names I had given him did not match the names on the file.

So whose was that birth certificate that I had found in the drawer?

And who am I?

★

The next step was to take the risk I was so afraid of taking and apply to the Home Office in the usual way, which meant visiting a social worker at the General Register Office in Southport, Lancashire.

Susie took the day off work to come with me and we agreed that I would travel up to London and meet her on the day, because it is better to sleep in your own bed the night before such things.

That morning the train I had intended to catch was cancelled, and the next train slowed and slowed with a faulty engine. The slower the train the faster my heart rate. And I had ended up sitting beside someone I knew vaguely, who talked more the less we moved.

I realised that by the time I reached Paddington I would have exactly fourteen minutes to get over to King's Cross. Impossible. This was London. It was at least twenty minutes in a taxi. There was only one hope and that was Virgin Limobikes – a motorbike taxi service I use.

As I ran out of Paddington Station the big bike was revved up. I jumped on the back and roared and veered through the London traffic, and although I am no pussycat, I had to close my eyes.

Eight minutes later I was on the platform with three minutes to go, and there was Susie – all five foot two of her – in her suede cowboy boots and beads, short skirt, rumpled hair and a Calvin Klein golden coat, looking kind-faced and gorgeous, but jamming her body in the doorway, and part-bossing part-flirting with the bemused guard, because she wasn't going to let the train leave till I was on it.

I fell through the door. The whistle blew.

We were on our way to the General Register Office with my passport and my two creased and crossed-out bits of paper – the court order and the Baby MOT. I had weighed 6 pounds 9 ounces.

Susie and I are sitting in a functional office of the kind recognisable anywhere in the world; fibreboard and veneer desk with metal legs, a low coffee table set round with ugly chairs semi-upholstered in Martian green and psychotic orange. Carpet tiles on the floor. A filing cabinet and a noticeboard. Big radiator. Bare window.

Susie is among the most skilled psychoanalysts in the world. She is smiling at me as the meeting begins, saying nothing, holding me in her mind. I could feel that very clearly.

The social worker I have come to see is a warm and spontaneous woman called Ria Hayward.

She talks for a while about data protection, and about the various UK Adoption Acts, and about the usual routes of contact. If I wanted to go further there were formalities. There always are.

She looks at my pieces of paper – the court order and the Baby MOT – and she notices that my mother had breastfed me.

'That was the one thing she could give you. She gave you what she could. She didn't have to do that and it would have been a lot easier for her if she hadn't. It is such a bond – breastfeeding. When she gave you up at six weeks old you were still part of her body.'

I do not want to cry. I am crying.

Then Ria passes me her own piece of paper with a sticker over it.

'This is the name of your birth mother, and this is your original name. I never look at it because I think the adopted person should see this first.'

I am standing up. I can't breathe.

'Is this it then?'

Susie and Ria are both smiling at me, as I take the paper over to the window. I read the names. Tears then. I don't know why. Why do we cry? The names read like runes.

Written on the body is a secret code only visible in certain lights.

Ria: 'I have counselled so many mothers over the years who are giving up their babies for adoption, and I tell you, Jeanette, they never want to do it. You were wanted – do you understand that?'

No. I have never felt wanted. I am the wrong crib.

'Do you understand that, Jeanette?'

No. And all my life I have repeated patterns of rejection. My success with my books felt like gatecrashing. When critics and the press turned on me, I roared back in rage, and no, I didn't believe the things they said about me or my work, because my writing has always stayed clear and luminous to me, uncontaminated, but I did know that I wasn't wanted.

And I have loved most extravagantly where my love could not be returned in any sane and steady way – the triangles of marriages and complex affiliations. I have failed to love well where I might have done, and I have stayed in relationships too long because I did not want to be a quitter who did not know how to love.

But I did not know how to love. If I could have faced that simple fact about myself, and the likelihood that someone with my story (my stories, both real and invented) would have big problems with love, then, then, what?

Listen, we are human beings. Listen, we are inclined to love. Love is there, but we need to be taught how. We want to stand upright, we want to walk, but someone needs to hold our hand and balance us a bit, and guide us a bit, and scoop us up when we fall.

Listen, we fall. Love is there but we have to learn it – and its shapes and its possibilities. I taught myself to stand on my own two feet, but I could not teach myself how to love.

We have a capacity for language. We have a capacity for love. We need other people to release those capacities.

In my work I found a way to talk about love – and that was real. I had not found a way to love. That was changing.

I am sitting in the room with Susie. She loves me. I want to accept it. I want to love well. I am thinking about the last two years and how I am trying my best to dissolve the calcifications around my heart.

Ria smiles and her voice comes from a long way off. All of this seems too present, because it is so uncomfortable, and too far away, because I can't focus. Ria smiles.

'*You were wanted, Jeanette.*'

★

On the train home Susie and I open half a bottle of Jim Beam bourbon. 'Affect regulation,' she says, and, as always with Susie, 'How are you feeling?'

In the economy of the body, the limbic highway takes precedence over the neural pathways. We were designed and built to feel, and there is no thought, no state of mind, that is not also a feeling state.

Nobody can feel too much, though many of us work very hard at feeling too little.

Feeling is frightening.

Well, I find it so.

The train was quiet in the exhausted way of late-home commuters. Susie was sitting opposite me, reading, her feet wrapped round my feet under the table. I keep running a Thomas Hardy poem through my head.

Never to bid good-bye
Or lip me the softest call,
Or utter a wish for a word, while I
Saw morning harden upon the wall,
Unmoved, unknowing
That your great going
Had place that moment, and altered all.

It was a poem I learned after Deborah left me, but the 'great going' had already happened at six weeks old.

The poem finds the word that finds the feeling.

★

Ria had given me the name of the court that might still hold my adoption records. Life was local in 1960, and while I had thought that I might be looking at somewhere in Manchester, it turned out that my records were in Accrington. I had walked past them every day of my life until I had left home.

I wrote a simple letter asking if the file had been kept.

A couple of weeks later I received a reply; yes, the file had been located, and now my request to see it would be placed before the judge.

I didn't like this; Ria had told me that it was my right to see the records, although no one could know what might or might not be there. Sometimes there is a lot of material, sometimes very little. Whatever else, I might find the name of the adoption society who had placed me with the Wintersons – the name that had been so violently torn off the top of the yellowing and faded Baby MOT.

I wanted to see those records. Who was this judge, this unknown male in authority? I was angry, but I knew enough to know that I was reaching into a very old radioactive anger.

Susie had gone to New York City and been marooned by the ash cloud that grounded all the aeroplanes across Europe and the Atlantic.

I was alone when another letter came from the court. The judge had spoken. 'Applicant should fill in the usual form and refer back.'

Get a solicitor, advised the letter.

I sat on the back step looking at it over and over again like someone who can't read. My body was slight-shaking all over in the way that you do if you get caught in an electric fence.

I went into the kitchen, picked up a plate, and threw it at the wall . . . 'Applicant . . . usual form . . . refer back . . .' It's not a fucking credit-card referral, you asshole.

And what happened next makes me ashamed but I will force myself to write it: I wet myself.

I don't know why or how. I know that I lost bladder control and that I sat down on the step soiled and wet and I couldn't get up to clean myself and I cried in the way that you do when there is nothing but crying.

There was nothing to hold on to. I wasn't Jeanette Winterson in her own home with books on the shelves and money in the bank; I was a baby and I was cold and wet and a judge had taken my mummy away.

Later, I'm dry and in clean clothes. I've had a drink. I ring Ria. She says, 'There is no usual form. You don't need a solicitor. This is mad. Leave it to me, Jeanette. I will help you.'

That night I lay on the bed thinking about what had happened.

This family court judge who was so experienced, did he have no idea of what it is like to stand on the rim of your life and look down into the crater?

How hard was it to send me the 'usual' form or to tell me where to download it, or have a court official talk me through the legalese?

I started shaking again.

★

'Lost loss' is unpredictable and not civilised. I was thrown back into a place of helplessness, powerlessness and despair. My body responded before my head. Normally, a pompous obfuscating letter from the legal world would make me laugh and I would just deal with it. I am not scared of lawyers and I know that the law is grandiose and designed to intimidate, even when there is no reason for it to do so. It is designed to make ordinary people feel inadequate. I do not feel inadequate – but I did not expect to be six weeks old again either.

Ria began to make enquiries and found that after the helpful simplicity of the opening meeting with her, the subsequent reality of dealing with the courts often proved too much. People gave up.

We decided that whatever else came of my search, we would try and formulate some guidelines for the courts and a road map for the clients, to make the process less awful.

An officer at the General Register Office who wanted to help me wrote directly to the court saying that I had already been identified by the Home Office, that she could verify me and my case, and that she would personally receive the file from the court.

No, said the judge. Not procedure.

I wondered what would have been expected of me if I had lived abroad? Would I have had to buy an air ticket and come and do this in a foreign place, unsupported, unless I bought two air tickets? What about all the post-war children who went to Australia? People's lives are less important than procedure . . .

★

Susie and I made an appointment at Accrington court.

In the waiting room were a row of miserable young men in badly fitting suits hoping to get off drink-driving offences. The girls were in full make-up looking defiant and scared over some shoplifting offence or public nuisance.

We were called into an interview room where lawyers can talk to their clients, and after a while, the court manager arrived, looking harassed and unhappy. I felt sorry for him.

He had an old file in one hand and a big fat book of procedure in the other. He knew I was going to be trouble.

In fact, I was so distressed at seeing the papers across the desk – the papers with all the details of my beginnings – that I could hardly speak at all. One of the saliencies of this retro adoption experience, these alienating legalities, is that I stumble on my words, hesitate, slow down and finally fall silent. The lost loss I experience as physical pain is pre-language. That loss happened before I could speak, and I return to that place, speechless.

Susie was charming, determined, relentless. The poor man was not sure what he could tell us and what he couldn't. There was so much I wanted to know – but the judge had not yet authorised the 'redacted' version. I was supposed to sign a few forms in person, go away, and wait for the papers to be sent on later.

But the file was on the table . . . not later . . . let it be now.

The court manager agreed that he could tell me

the name of the adoption society. That was a very useful piece of information. He wrote it on a piece of paper and he photocopied the original in the clerk's handwriting – oh it looks so old. The forms he is holding are yellow and handwritten.

Is my mother's date of birth there? That would help me to find her. He shakes his head. He can't tell me that.

All right then, listen, my adoptive mother, Mrs Winterson, always said my birth mother was seventeen. If I knew her age I could start using the ancestry site to find her – but her name is common enough, and although I have narrowed it down to two likely possibilities, I don't know which one to follow. And both could be wrong. This is the forking path. This is where the universe divides. Help me.

He is sweating. He is looking in the procedure book. Susie tells me to leave the room.

I bang out through the swing doors onto the pavement with remnants of the youth, some of whom are looking cocky and relieved, some are in despair, they are all smoking and talking at once.

I wish I wasn't here. I wish I hadn't started this. Why did I start it?

And I am back to the locked box with the Royal Albert in it, and the papers hidden beneath, and further back the wrong birth certificate, and who was the woman who came to the door and frightened Mrs Winterson into tears and rage?

When I go back in Susie has extracted a promise from the court manager that he will go and ask the judge in session just what he can or can't tell me from the file. We have to come back in forty-five minutes.

So we walk away and sit outside a caff that serves big mugs of tea and I realise that this place doing burgers and chips used to be the Palatine, beloved of Mrs W and the beans on toast and the fugged-up windows of my future on the mission fields.

'I had to send you out to shut you up,' said Susie. I look at her in amazement. I thought I had been completely silent. 'Don't you remember what you said? It wasn't actually anything. It was just babble, the poor guy!'

But I don't babble! And my mind is blank – not a bit blank, totally blank – I am obviously going insane again. I should stop this whole thing now. I hate being in Accrington. I don't want to remember any of this.

I haven't been here since Dad's funeral.

Throughout my mad time/bad time, I had driven up to Lancashire once a month to visit Dad and he had come to stay with me in the country. He was getting weaker all the time but he loved the visits, and in 2008 he was coming for Christmas.

I arranged for Dad to be driven down and he sat in front of the fire looking out of the window. He had been advised by the doctor not to travel but he was determined to come and I was determined too, and I had spoken to his doctor who told me that Dad was hardly eating.

When he arrived I asked him very gently if he wanted to die, and he smiled at me and said, 'After Christmas.'

It was and it wasn't a joke. On Christmas night I

realised I would never get him into bed and so I made up the cushions in front of the fire and half pulled half pushed him from the chair onto this makeshift but comfortable bed, undressing him as I did so, and getting him into his pyjamas. He fell straight asleep in the dying firelight and I sat with him, talking to him, telling him I wished we could have got it right sooner, but that it was a good thing, a glad thing, that we had got it right at all.

I went to bed and woke up bolt upright at around 4 a.m. and came downstairs. The cats were lying on Dad's bed, very calm, and Dad was breathing shallowly but he was breathing.

The sky was full of stars and at that time of day/ night they are lower and nearer. I opened the curtains to let in the stars, in case Dad woke, in this world or some other.

He didn't die that night and two days later Steve from the church came to drive him back to Accrington. As they set off, I realised that in all the fuss of suitcases and mince pies and presents, I hadn't said goodbye, so I jumped into my Land Rover and chased after them, but as I came up behind them at the traffic light on the hill, the lights changed rapidly, and they were gone.

The next day Dad died.

I drove up to Accrington to the care home. Dad was laid out in his room, beautifully shaved and groomed. Nesta, the owner, had done it herself. 'I like to do it,' she said. 'It's my way. Sit with him while I get you some tea.'

There used to be a tradition in the north of England

that if you wanted to show respect you served tea in tiny cups. Nesta, who is a giantess, came back with tea in a doll's house set including sugar tongs the size of eyebrow tweezers. She sat in the one chair and I sat on the divan with Dead Dad.

'You'll have to see the coroner,' she said. 'You might have poisoned him.'

'Poisoned my dad?'

'Yes. With a mince pie. The doctor told him not to travel – he comes to you alive – he comes back here and drops dead. I blame Harold Shipman.'

Harold Shipman was the most recent in a line of macabre doctors to have killed off a large number of elderly patients. But he hadn't killed off Dad.

'I mean,' said Nesta, 'that they look at everything now. The coroner will have to release the body before we can bury your dad. I tell you that Harold Shipman has ruined it for us all.'

She poured more tea and smiled at Dad. 'Look at him. He's with us. You can tell.'

The coroner did release the body but the moments of black comedy were not over. Dad had a burial plot, but after the funeral service, and when we had arrived at the cemetery, my cheque payment to open the grave had not arrived. The grave was ready but the cemetery wanted the cash. I went into the office and asked what to do. One of the men started explaining where I could find the nearest cashpoint. I said, 'My father is outside in his coffin. I cannot go to the cashpoint.'

'Well, we normally do insist on pre-payment because once somebody is buried you can't just dig them up if the relatives do a bunk.'

I tried to assure them that I was not going to do a bunk. Fortunately I had a copy of *Oranges* in my handbag – I was going to put it in Dad's coffin but I changed my mind. They were quite impressed by the book and one of them had seen it on the telly, so . . . after a bit of shuffling they agreed to take another cheque on the spot, and my father in his willow coffin was lowered down into the grave he shares with his second wife. That was his wish.

Mrs Winterson lies further off. Alone.

It was time to go back to the court. 'Just keep your mouth shut,' said Susie.

The court manager was looking a lot more cheerful. He had been authorised by the judge to confirm my mother's age, though not her date of birth. She had been seventeen. So Mrs Winterson had told the truth about that.

I took Susie to see my house, 200 Water Street, and the Elim Church on Blackburn Road, and the library, now shamefully stripped of so many of its books, including English Literature A–Z.

Like most libraries in the UK, books are now less important than computer terminals and CD loans.

Then we drove back to Manchester, passing Blackley, where my mother used to live. Was she there now? Was that woman at the bus stop her?

Mrs Winterson had told me she was dead. True? Not true?

★

The adoption society had long since vanished, and now there was yet another mouldering file to be found. I telephoned the new authority and, half stumbling, half babbling, gave my details.

'What is your name?'

'Jeanette Winterson.'

'No, your name at birth. That will be on our records not Winterson. Did you write that book *Oranges Are Not the Only Fruit*?'

Nightmare nightmare nightmare.

I leave them to deal with the archive and settle down to investigate the ancestry site.

I am terminally uninterested in record-keeping. I burn my work in progress and I burn my diaries, and I destroy letters. I don't want to sell my working papers to Texas and I don't want my personal papers becoming doctoral theses. I don't understand the family tree obsession. But then I wouldn't, would I?

My website explorations led me to believe that my mother had married after I was adopted. My father's name was not on my birth certificate so I had no idea whether the two of them began a new life together, a fresh start, or whether she was pushed into a life with someone else.

Either way I took an instant and unjustified dislike to the man she married, praying that he is not my father. His name is not Pierre K. King but it is a name like that, in its Frenchified absurdity.

Then to my relief, I found that he and my mother were divorced quite quickly, and that he died in 2009.

But I discovered that I have a brother, or at least a half-brother, and had better not be too rude about the dad, who may or may not be my dad.

What made them give me away? It had to be his fault because I couldn't let it be hers. I had to believe that my mother loved me. That was risky. That could be a fantasy. If I had been wanted why had I become unwanted six weeks later?

And I wondered if a lot of my negativity towards men in general was tied up with these lost beginnings.

I don't feel negative about men any more – that was something else that shifted decisively when I was going mad. The men I knew were kind to me, and I found I could rely on them. But my change of heart was more than specific; it was a larger compassion for all the suffering and inadequacies of human beings, male or female.

But new JW or not – I was very angry with my mother's husband. I wanted to kill him even though he was dead.

No word from the adoption society. I had to shout at myself before I could call again. Dialing the number makes me pace and it makes me breathless.

They are all very nice – sorry – they lost my phone number. Oh, and I can't see the file, but my social worker can, providing she gives me no details about the Wintersons, which is an odd rule I think, especially when they are both dead.

Ria writes to ask for the file, and meanwhile it is my birthday, and meanwhile I have lost track of my mother, because women change their names. Has she married again? Is she alive?

That worries me. All this effort and perhaps she is dead. I always believed she was dead . . . A Mrs W story.

Susie and I are flying to New York City on my birthday. Susie says, 'I think you do know how to love.'

'Do I?'

'I don't think you know how to be loved.'

'What do you mean?'

'Most women can give – we're trained to it – but most women find it hard to receive. You are generous and you are kind – I wouldn't want to be with you otherwise, no matter how brainy and impressive you are – but our conflicts and our difficulties revolve round love. You don't trust me to love you, do you?'

No . . . I am the wrong crib . . . this will go wrong like all the rest. In my heart of hearts I believe that.

The love-work that I have to do now is to believe that life will be all right for me. I don't have to be alone. I don't have to fight for everything. I don't have to fight everything. I don't have to run away. I can stay because this is love that is offered, a sane steady stable love.

'And if we have to part,' says Susie, 'you will know that you were in a good relationship.'

You are wanted, do you understand that, Jeanette?

Ria and I are meeting in Liverpool where she lives. She arrives at my hotel with yet another envelope and I feel that familiar dryness and heart race.

We get a drink. Out comes another ancient form.

'Well,' says Ria, 'full working–class credentials – your

199

dad was a miner! And only five feet two inches tall
– look, someone has written that in pencil on the
back. He was keen on sport. He was twenty-one.
Dark hair.'

And he isn't Pierre K. King! Rejoice!

I think about my own body. I am only five feet
tall exactly – and the genetic rule is that girls are not
taller than their fathers, so I have done all I can
size-wise.

I have a strong upper body – the kind bred to
crawl in low tunnels and pull carts of coal around
and work heavy hand-held kit. I can pick up Susie
easily – partly because I go to the gym, but also
because my power ratio is in my top half. And I always
had a bad chest . . . the miner's inheritance.

And I am thinking that in 1985, the year that I
published *Oranges*, Margaret Thatcher was smashing
the National Union of Mineworkers for ever. Was my
dad on the picket lines?

On the form is my mother's date of birth at last
– she's a Sagittarius, and so is my dad.

The form says Reason for Adoption. My mother
has handwriten, *Better for Janet to have a mother and a
father.*

I know from my dives into the ancestry website
that her own father died when she was eight. And I
know that she was one of ten children.

Better for Janet to have a mother and a father.

So I was Janet – not so far from Jeanette – but
Mrs Winterson was the one who Frenchified it. Yeah,
she just would . . .

'I am not allowed to tell you much about the
Wintersons,' said Ria, 'The information here is

confidential, but there are letters from Mrs Winterson saying that she hopes to be able to adopt a baby, and there is a note from the social worker who visited them reporting that the outside toilet is clean and in good order . . . and a little note that says of your future mum and dad, "not what one would call modern".'

Ria and I fall about laughing – that note was 1959. They were not modern then, how could they ever catch up when the 1960s happened?

'And there's something else,' said Ria. 'Are you ready?'

No. I am not ready for any of this. Let's have another drink. At that moment in comes a theatre director I know slightly – she is staying at the hotel – and soon we are all three having drinks and chatting away, and I wish I was one of those cartoon characters with a saw coming up through the floor in a big circle round my chair.

Time passes.

Are you ready?

'There was another baby . . . before you . . . a boy . . . Paul.'

Paul? My saintly invisible brother Paul? The boy they could have had. The one who would never have drowned his doll in the pond, or filled his pyjama case with tomatoes. The Devil led us to the wrong crib. Are we back at the beginning? And was the birth certificate I found, in fact, Paul's?

Ria doesn't know what happened to Paul, but there is a note from Mrs Winterson that I am not allowed to see, expressing great disappointment, and explaining that she had already bought Paul's baby clothes and wouldn't be able to afford a new set.

I am just about beginning to take in that Mrs Winterson was expecting a boy, and that as she couldn't afford to waste the clothes, I would have been dressed as a boy . . . So I started life not as Janet, not as Jeanette, but as Paul.

Oh no oh no oh no, and I thought my life was all about sexual choice and feminism and and . . . it turns out I began as a boy.

Ask not for whom the bell tolls.

There is such fierce humour in this absurd explanation for everything that my feelings for all my mothers and all my identities are suddenly joyful not fearful. Life is ridiculous. Chaotic crazy life. And I am reciting in my head the Anne Sexton poem – the last one in her collection *The Awful Rowing Toward God* (1975). It's the one called 'The Rowing Endeth'. She sits down with God and . . .

> *'On with it!' He says and thus*
> *we squat on the rocks by the sea*
> *and play – can it be true –*
> *a game of poker.*
> *He calls me.*
> *I win because I hold a royal straight flush.*
> *He wins because He holds five aces*
> *A wild card had been announced*
> *but I had not heard it*
> *being in such a state of awe*
> *when He took out the cards and dealt.*
> *As He plunks down His five aces*
> *and I sit grinning at my royal flush,*

He starts to laugh,
the laughter rolling like a hoop out of His mouth
and into mine,
and such laughter that He doubles right over me
laughing a Rejoice-Chorus at our two triumphs.
Then I laugh, the fishy dock laughs
the sea laughs. The Island laughs.
The Absurd laughs.

Dearest dealer,
I with my royal straight flush,
love you so for your wild card,
that untamable, eternal, gut-driven ha-ha
and lucky love.

And lucky love. Yes. Always.

Susie tells me that mothers do everything with boy babies differently – they handle them differently and they talk to them differently. She believes that if Mrs W had psychologically prepared herself for a boy through the long process of waiting to adopt, she would not have been able to shift her internal gear when she got a girl. And I, sensitive to all signals, because I was trying to survive a loss, would be trying to negotiate what was being offered and what was being required.

I want to say that I don't think identity or sexual identity is fixed in this way, but I think it makes sense to factor in what happened to me – especially as Mrs Winterson must have had enough confusion for both of us.

She was always lamenting that I would not be

parted from my shorts – but who put them on me in the first place?

I felt freed by the new information but I was no nearer to finding my mother.

I was lucky because a friend of mine has a cryptic crossword kind of mind, and he loves computers. He was determined to find me a family tree, and spent hours logged onto the ancestry site looking for clues. He targeted male relatives because men don't change their surnames.

Eventually he made a direct hit – an uncle of mine. He used the Electoral Register to find the address. Then he tracked the phone number. For three weeks I rehearsed the call. I had to have a cover story.

One Saturday morning, heart beating like a dying bird, I called. A man answered.

I said, 'Hello – you don't know me but your sister and my mother were very close at one time.'

Well, that was true, wasn't it?

'Which sister?' he said. 'Ann or Linda?'

'Ann.'

'Oh Ann. What did you say your name was? Are you trying to get in touch with her?'

My mother was alive.

My feelings as I put down the phone were a mixture of elation and fear. Mrs Winterson had lied; my mother wasn't dead. But that meant I had a mother. And my whole identity was built around being an orphan – and an only child. But now I had a selection of uncles and aunts . . . and who knew how many bits of brothers and sisters?

I decided to write a letter to Ann and to send it care of the uncle.

About a week later there was a text on my phone from an unidentified number. It was headed 'Darling Girl'. I thought it was from a Russian escort agency and was about to delete it. A work colleague had had their computer stolen and ever since I had been receiving mad messages from Baltic lovelies looking for husbands.

Susie grabbed the phone. 'Suppose it's from Ann?'

'Of course it's not from Ann!' I opened it – the trouble is that the Baltic lovelies all began with things like 'Can't believe it's you . . .' and so did this.

'Do you want me to ring the number?' said Susie.

Yes. No. Yes. No. Yes. No. Yes.

Susie went downstairs with my phone and I did what I always do when I am overwhelmed – I went straight to sleep.

Susie came back upstairs to find me snoring. She shook me awake. 'That was your mother.'

And a few days later, a letter arrived, with a photo of me at three weeks old – looking pretty worried I think. But Susie says that all babies look worried – and who can blame us?

The letter tells me how she was sixteen when she got pregnant – my father had jet-black hair. How she looked after me for six weeks in a mother and baby home before she gave me up. 'That was so hard. But I had no money and nowhere to go.'

She tells me I was never a secret – me – who

thought via Mrs Winterson that everything had to be secret – books and lovers, real names, real lives.

And then she wrote, 'You were always wanted.'

Do you understand that, Jeanette? You were always wanted.

14

Strange Meeting

. . . my mother came running down the street after me. Look at her, like an angel, like a light-beam, running alongside the pram. I lifted up my hands to catch her, and the light was there, the outline of her, but like angels and light she vanished.

Is that her, at the end of the street, smaller and smaller, like a light-years-away star?

I always believed I would see her again.

The Stone Gods (2007)

I WAS TALKING TO MY friend the film director Beeban Kidron. She directed *Oranges* for TV, and we have known each other a long time. We have both been volatile and difficult people – with each other as well as with many others – but we have both arrived at some sort of settlement with life; not a compromise, a settlement.

We were laughing about Mrs Winterson and how monstrous and impossible she was, but how absolutely right for someone like me, who, like her, could never have accepted a scaled-down life. She turned inwards; I turned outwards.

'What would you have been without her?' said

Beeban. 'I know you were impossible, but at least you did something with it. Imagine if you had just been impossible!'

Yes . . . I had an unsettling experience in Manchester. I had opened an exhibition of women surrealists at the Manchester Art Gallery, and late at night I found myself with the sponsors in a bar.

It was one of those bars that used to be a basement for the rubbish, but loadsamoney Manchester, the original alchemical city, was turning all its dross into gold. Why store bin bags in your cellar when you could flood it with blue light, ship in a pyramid of leggy chrome stools, cover the crappy walls with distorting mirrors, and charge twenty quid for a vodka Martini?

A very special vodka Martini of course, made from potato vodka in a smoke-blue bottle and personally mixed before your eyes by a camp barman with good hand movements.

That night I was wearing a pinstripe Armani skirt suit, a pink vest, Jimmy Choos, and – for reasons I can't go into here – I had a spray tan.

I suddenly realised that I would always have been in this bar that night. If I hadn't found books, if I hadn't turned my oddness into poetry and the anger into prose, well, I wasn't ever going to be a nobody with no money. I would have used the Manchester magic to make an alchemy of my own.

I'd have gone into property and made a fortune. I'd have had a boob job by now, and be on my second or third husband, and live in a ranch-style house with a Range Rover on the gravel and a hot tub in the garden, and my kids wouldn't be speaking to me.

I'd still be in the Armani, with the spray tan, drinking too many of these vodka Martinis in too many of these blue basement bars.

I am the kind of person who would rather walk than wait for a bus. The kind of person who will drive out of my way rather than sit in traffic. The kind of person who assumes that any problem is there for me to solve. I am not capable of queuing – I'd rather give up on whatever I have to queue for – and I won't take no for an answer. What is 'no'? Either you have asked the wrong question or you have asked the wrong person. Find a way to get the 'yes'.

'You need to get to the "yes",' said Beeban. 'Some sort of yes to who you were and that means settling the backstory. I don't know why you do, after all this time, but you do.'

I suppose it is because of the forking paths. I keep seeing my life darting off in the different directions it could have taken, as chance and circumstance, temperament and desire, open and close, open and close gates, routes, roadways.

And yet there feels like an inevitability to who I am – just as of all the planets in all the universes, planet blue, this planet Earth, is the one that is home.

I guess that over the last few years I have come home. I have always tried to make a home for myself, but I have not felt at home in myself. I have worked hard at being the hero of my own life, but every time I checked the register of displaced persons, I was still on it. I didn't know how to belong.

Longing? Yes. Belonging? No.

★

Ruth Rendell called me. 'I think you should just go and get it over with. Now that you have found your mother you must see her. Have you spoken to her on the phone?'

'No'

'Why ever not?'

'I am scared.'

'There'd be something wrong with you if you weren't scared!'

I trust Ruth and I (nearly) always do what she tells me. It was unlike her to ring me up and quiz me but she had a feeling I was running away from this. And I was. I had spent a year bringing this moment nearer and nearer and now I was stalling for time.

'What train will you get?'

'All right . . . All right.'

All right. So in spite of the snow and in spite of the fact that the TV news was telling us all to stay at home, I took a train to Manchester. I decided to stay the night in a hotel and get a taxi to see Ann the next morning.

I like the hotel and I often stay there. I stayed there the night before my father's funeral.

The next day as my father's coffin was carried into the church I broke down. I had not been in that church for thirty-five years and suddenly everything was present again; the old present.

When I stood up to speak about Dad, I said, 'The things that I regret in my life are not errors of judgement but failures of feeling.'

210

I was thinking about that as I ate my dinner quietly in my room.

There is still a popular fantasy, long since disproved by both psychoanalysis and science, and never believed by any poet or mystic, that it is possible to have a thought without a feeling. It isn't.

When we are objective we are subjective too. When we are neutral we are involved. When we say 'I think' we don't leave our emotions outside the door. To tell someone not to be emotional is to tell them to be dead.

My own failures of feeling were a consequence of closing down feeling where it had become too painful. I remember watching *Toy Story 3* with my godchildren, and crying when the abandoned bear turned playroom tyrant sums up his survivor-philosophy: 'No owner, no heartbreak.'

But I wanted to be claimed.

I had styled myself as the Lone Ranger not Lassie. What I had to understand is that you can be a loner *and* want to be claimed. We're back to the complexity of life that isn't this thing or that thing – the boring old binary oppositions – it's both, held in balance. So simple to write. So hard to do/be.

And the people I have hurt, the mistakes I have made, the damage to myself and others, wasn't poor judgement; it was the place where love had hardened into loss.

I am in a taxi going out of Manchester. I have flowers. I have the address. I feel terrible. Susie calls me. 'Where are you?' *No idea, Susie.* 'How long have you been in the cab?' *About fifty years.*

Manchester is either bling or damage. The warehouses and civic buildings have become hotels and bars or fancy apartments. The centre of Manchester is noisy, shiny, brash, successful, flaunting its money as it always did from the moment it became the engine of England.

Travel out further, and the changing fortunes of Manchester are evident. The decent rows of solid terraces have been slum-cleared and replaced with tower blocks and cul-de-sacs, shopping compounds and gaming arcades. Indian cash-and-carry outlets seem to make a living, but most of the small shops are boarded up, lost on fast, hostile roads.

Now and again, forlorn and marooned, there's a four-square stone building that says Mechanics' Institute or Co-operative Society. There's a viaduct, a cluster of birch trees, a blackened stone wall; the remains of the remains. A tyre warehouse, a giant supermarket, a minicab sign, a betting shop, kids on skateboards who have never known life any other way. Old men with bewildered faces. How did we get here?

I feel the same anger I feel when I go back to my home town twenty miles away. Who funds municipal vandalism and why? Why can decent people not live in decent environments? Why is it tarmac and metal railings, ugly housing estates and retail parks?

I love the industrial north of England and I hate what has happened to it.

But I know these thoughts are my own way of distracting myself. The taxi is slowing down. This is it, JW. We're here.

As I get out of the cab I feel trapped, desperate, desperately frightened and physically sick. Susie has always said to me to be in the feeling and not to push it away, however difficult.

I have a hysterical impulse to sing 'Cheer Up Ye Saints of God'. But no, that's the other childhood, the other mother.

The door opens before I knock. There's a man there who does look rather like me. I know I have a half-brother so this must be him. 'Gary?' I say. 'Hello, sister,' says Gary.

And then there's a scuffle from the kitchen and two tiny dogs appear bouncing up and down like hairy yo-yos, and from a tangle with the washing line, which at below-freezing temperatures shows true optimism, in comes my mother.

She is small, bright-eyed, with an open smile.

I am very pleased to see her. 'I thought I'd get the washing done before you got here,' is her very first line.

It is just what I would say myself.

Ann knows about my life. I sent her the DVD of *Oranges* as a kind of 'This is what happened while you were out'. She feels distress at Winterson-world and my other mother's flamboyant craziness upsets her. 'I'm sorry I left you. I didn't want to, you know that, don't you? I had no money and nowhere to go and Pierre wouldn't bring up another man's child.'

I had thought as much . . . but I didn't say anything because it didn't seem fair to Gary for his new half-sister just-arrived to start laying into his deceased dad.

I don't want her to be upset. 'I don't mind,' I said.

Later, when I relay this to Susie, she decides, when she can stop laughing, that this is the world's most

213

inadequate response. 'I don't mind? Just put me on the step until the van with the Gospel Tent comes by. I don't mind!'

But, it's true . . . I don't mind. I certainly don't blame her. I think she did the only thing she could do. I was her message in a bottle thrown overboard.

And I do know, really know, that Mrs W gave me what she could too – it was a dark gift but not a useless one.

My mother is straightforward and kind. This feels odd to me. A female parent is meant to be labyrinth-like and vengeful. I have been worried about declaring the girlfriend because Ann has already asked me about a husband and children. But the girlfriend must be declared.

'Do you mean you don't go with men?' she says.

And I suppose that is what I mean.

'I have no problem with that,' says Ann.

'Me neither,' says Gary.

Hold on . . . that's not what's supposed to happen . . . what's supposed to happen is as follows:

I am determined to tell Mrs Winterson that I am in love. I am no longer living at home but I would like her to understand how it is for me. I will be going to Oxford soon and enough time has passed from the happy/normal moment. That's what I think, but I am learning that time is unreliable. Those old sayings about Give It Time, and Time is a Healer depend on just whose time it is. As Mrs Winterson lives in End Time, ordinary time doesn't mean much to her. She is still indignant about the wrong crib.

She is polishing the coal scuttle with Brasso. She has already polished the flying ducks over the mantelpiece and the crocodile nutcracker. I have no idea how to begin so I open my mouth and I say, 'I think I am always going to love women in the way that I do . . .'

At that instant her varicose vein in the top of her leg bursts. It goes up like a geezer and hits the ceiling in a crimson splash. I grab the Brasso cloths and I am trying to stem the flow . . . 'I'm sorry. I didn't want to upset you . . .' Then her leg erupts again.

By now she is lying backwards in the chair with her leg up on the half-polished coal scuttle. She is looking at the ceiling. She doesn't say anything.

'Mum . . . are you all right?'

'We've just had that ceiling decorated.'

What would my life have been like if she had said, 'Oh, your dad and I don't have a problem with that'?

What would my life have been like if I had been with Ann? Would I have had a girlfriend? And what if I hadn't had to fight for a girlfriend, fight for myself? I am not a big believer in the gay gene. Maybe I would have got married, had the kids, and then gone off to get the spray tan, etc.

I must have fallen silent, thinking about all this.

Ann says, 'Was Mrs Winterson a latent lesbian?'

I choke on my tea. That is like Burn a Koran Day. There are some things you can't even suggest. But now that it has been suggested I am overwhelmed by the awful thought. I am pretty sure she wasn't a latent anything – it might have been better if some of her tendencies could have been latent. I suppose she might have been a latent murderer, what with the revolver in the duster drawer, etc., but I think it was all on the surface with her, just hopelessly scrambled. She was her own Enigma Code and me and my dad were not Bletchley Park.

'I just wondered,' said Ann, 'what with her saying, "Never let a boy touch you down there."'

'She didn't want me to get pregnant.' Oh dear. Not the right thing to say, but then Mrs Winterson was dead set against illegitimacy as it used to be called, and had nothing but contempt for the woman who gave me my chance at life and Mrs Winterson her chance at me.

'I have had four husbands,' said Ann.

'Four?'

She smiles. She doesn't judge herself and she doesn't judge others. Life is as it is.

My father the miniature miner from Manchester was not one of the four.

'You've got his shape, narrow hips, we've all got wide hips, and you've got his hair. He was really dark. Very good-looking. He was a Teddy boy.'

I have to think about this. My mother has had four husbands. My other mother might have been a latent lesbian. My father was a Teddy boy. It is a lot to take in.

'I like men myself, but I don't rely on them. I can do my own electrics, my own plastering and I can put up a shelf. I don't rely on anybody, me.'

Yes, we are alike. The optimism, the self-reliance. The ease we both have in our bodies. I used to wonder why I have always felt at ease in my body and liked my body. I look at her and it seems to be an inheritance.

Gary is well built but compact. He loves walking. He thinks nothing of walking fourteen miles on a Saturday afternoon. He boxes too. They have kept their working-class pride in who they are and what they can do. They like each other. I watch that. They talk. I listen to that. Is this what it would have been like?

But Ann had to work all the time because Pierre left her when the boys were little. And I suppose I would have had to look after my brothers. And I would have resented that.

I remember what she wrote on the adoption form. *Better for Janet to have a mother and a father.*

But her sons didn't have a father at home for long. And neither did she. Her own father died in the 1950s.

'There were ten of us,' said Ann. 'How did we fit into two bedrooms? And we were always doing a flit when we couldn't pay the rent. My dad had a handcart and he'd come back and shout, "Pack up, we're off," and what we had went in the handcart and we started again. There were a lot of cheap places to rent in those days.'

My maternal grandmother bore ten children, two died in infancy, four are left. She worked all her life, and when she wasn't working she was a ballroom-dancing champion.

'And she lived to be ninety-seven,' said Ann.

I go to the bathroom. All my life I have been an orphan and an only child. Now I come from a big noisy family who go ballroom dancing and live forever.

Ann's youngest sister Linda arrives. She is technically my aunt, but she is the same age as my girlfriend, and it is ludicrous to be collecting aunts at this stage in life.

'Everybody wants to meet you,' says Linda. 'I saw *Oranges* on the TV but I didn't know it was you. My daughter has ordered all your books.'

That shows willing. We have all got adjustments to make.

I like Linda, who lives in Spain, where she runs women's groups and teaches dancing, among other things. 'I'm the quiet one,' she says. 'You can't get a word in edgeways when that lot are all together.'

'We should have a party,' says Ann. Then she says, with an almost Mrs W-style segue, 'Every morning I wake up and I ask myself, "Why am I here?"'

She doesn't mean 'Oh no, I am still here' – it isn't quite Mrs W. She really wants the question answered.

'There must be a meaning but we don't know it,' says Gary. 'I'm always reading about the cosmos.'

Linda has been reading *The Tibetan Book of Living and Dying*, which she recommends to Gary.

This is the old Manchester working-class way; you think, you read, you ponder. We could be back in the Mechanics' Institute, back in the Workers' Extension Lectures, back in the Public Library Reading Room. I feel proud – of them, of me, of our past, our heritage. And I feel very sad. I shouldn't be the only one to have been educated. Everyone in this room is intelligent. Everyone in this room is thinking about the bigger questions. Try telling that to the Utility educators.

I don't know why we are here either, but whatever

the answers, I'm back with Engels in 1844. We're not here to be regarded 'only as useful objects'.

They are easy to talk to. Five hours pass very quickly indeed. But I have to go. I have to get to London. Susie will meet me. I stand up to say goodbye. My legs are weak. I am exhausted.

Ann hugs me. 'I wondered if you would ever try and find me. I hoped you would. I wanted to find you but it didn't seem right to try.'

I am not able to say what I want to say. I can't think straight. I hardly notice the taxi ride back to the station. I grab some food for me and Susie, because she's been working all day, and I get myself half a bottle of red wine. I try and phone Susie but I can't speak. 'Read the paper. Chill. You are in shock.'

There's a text from Ann. *I hope you weren't disappointed.*

15

The Wound

M_{Y MOTHER HAD TO SEVER} some part of herself to let me go. I have felt the wound ever since.

Mrs Winterson was such a mix of truth and fraud. She invented many bad mothers for me; fallen women, drug addicts, drinkers, men-chasers. The other mother had a lot to carry but I carried it for her, wanting to defend her and feeling ashamed of her all at the same time.

The hardest part was not knowing.

I have always been interested in stories of disguise and mistaken identity, of naming and knowing. How are you recognised? How do you recognise yourself?

In the *Odyssey*, Odysseus, for all his adventures and far-flung wandering, is always urged to 'remember the return'. The journey is about coming home.

When he reaches Ithaca the place is in uproar with unruly suitors for his hard-pressed wife. Two things happen: his dog scents him, and his wife recognises him by the scar on his thigh.

She feels the wound.

There are so many wound stories:

Chiron, the centaur, half-man, half-horse, is shot by a poisoned arrow tipped in the Hydra's blood, and because he is immortal and cannot die, he must live forever in agony. But he uses the pain of the wound to heal others. The wound becomes its own salve.

Prometheus, fire-stealer from the gods, is punished with a daily wound: each morning an eagle perches on his hip and rips out his liver; each night the wound heals, only to be scored open the next day. I think of him, burned dark in the sun where he is chained to the Caucausian mountains, the skin on his stomach as soft and pale as a little child's.

The doubting disciple Thomas must put his hand into the spear-wound in Jesus' side, before he can accept that Jesus is who he says he is.

Gulliver, finishing his travels, is wounded by an arrow in the back of the knee as he leaves the country of the Houyhnhnms – the gentle and intelligent horses, far superior to humankind.

On his return home Gulliver prefers to live in his own stables, and the wound behind his knee never heals. It is the reminder of another life.

One of the most mysterious wounds is in the story of the Fisher King. The King is keeper of the Grail, and is sustained by it, but he has a wound that will not heal, and until it does heal, the kingdom cannot be united. Eventually Galahad comes and lays hands on the King. In other versions it is Perceval.

The wound is symbolic and cannot be reduced to any single interpretation. But wounding seems to be a clue or a key to being human. There is value here as well as agony.

What we notice in the stories is the nearness of the wound to the gift: the one who is wounded is marked out – literally and symbolically – by the wound. The wound is a sign of difference. Even Harry Potter has a scar.

Freud colonised the Oedipus myth and renamed it as the son who kills the father and desires the mother. But Oedipus is an adoption story and a wound story too. Oedipus has his ankles pierced together by his mother Jocasta before she abandons him, so that he cannot crawl away. He is rescued, and returns to kill his father and marry his mother, unrecognised by anyone except the blind prophet Tiresias – a case of one wound recognising another.

You cannot disown what is yours. Flung out, there is always the return, the reckoning, the revenge, perhaps the reconciliation.

There is always the return. And the wound will take you there. It is a blood-trail.

As the cab pulls up outside the house it starts to snow. When I was going mad I had a dream that I was lying face down on a sheet of ice and underneath me, hand to hand, mouth to mouth, was another me, ice-trapped.

I want to break the ice, but will I stab myself?

Standing in the snow, I could be standing at any point on the line of my past. I was bound to get here.

Birthing is a wound all of its own. The monthly bleeding used to have a magical significance. The baby's rupture into the world tears the mother's body and leaves the child's tiny skull still soft and open. The child is a healing and a cut. The place of lost and found.

It's snowing. Here I am. Lost and Found.

★

What stands before me now like a stranger I think I recognise, is love. The return, or rather the returning, named the 'lost loss'. I could not smash the ice that separated me from myself, I could only let it melt, and that meant losing all firm foothold, all sense of ground. It meant a chaotic merging with what felt like utter craziness.

All my life I have worked from the wound. To heal it would mean an end to one identity – the defining identity. But the healed wound is not the disappeared wound; there will always be a scar. I will always be recognisable by my scar.

And so will my mother, whose wound it is too, and who has had to shape a life around a choice she did not want to make. Now, from now on, how do we know each other? Are we mother and daughter? What are we?

Mrs Winterson was gloriously wounded, like a medieval martyr, gouged and dripping for Jesus, and she dragged her cross for all to see. Suffering was the meaning of life. If you had said, 'Why are we here?' She would have replied, 'To suffer.'

After all, in End Time, this vestibule existence of life on earth can only be a succession of losses.

But my other mother had lost me and I had lost her, and our other life was like a shell on the beach that holds an echo of the sea.

Who was it then, the figure who came into the garden all those years ago and threw Mrs Winterson into rage and pain and sent me flying down the hall, knocked back into the other life?

I suppose it might have been Paul's mother, the saintly invisible Paul. I suppose I might have imagined it. But that is not my feeling. Whatever happened that violent afternoon was tied to the birth certificate that I found, but it turned out not to be mine, and tied to the years and years later opening of the box – its own kind of fate – where I found the pieces of paper that told me I had another name – crossed out.

I have learned to read between the lines. I have learned to see behind the image.

Back in the days of Winterson-world we had a set of Victorian watercolours hung on the walls. Mrs W had inherited them from her mother and she wanted to display them in a family way. But she was dead against 'graven images' (See Exodus, Leviticus, Deuteronomy, etc.), so she squared this circle by hanging them back to front. All we could see was brown paper, tape, steel tacks, water-staining and string. That was a Mrs Winterson version of life.

'I ordered your book from the library,' said Ann, 'before you sent me anything, and I said to the librarian, "This is my daughter." "What?" she said. "It's for your daughter?" "No! Jeanette Winterson is my daughter." I felt so proud.'

Phone box 1985. Mrs Winterson in her headscarf in a rage.

The pips . . . more money in the slot . . . and I'm thinking, 'Why aren't you proud of me?'

224

The pips . . . more money in the slot . . . 'It's the first time I've had to order a book in a false name.'

Happy endings are only a pause. There are three kinds of big endings: Revenge. Tragedy. Forgiveness. Revenge and Tragedy often happen together. Forgiveness redeems the past. Forgiveness unblocks the future.

My mother tried to throw me clear of her own wreckage and I landed in a place as unlikely as any she could have imagined for me.

There I am, leaving her body, leaving the only thing I know, and repeating the leaving again and again until it is my own body I am trying to leave, the last escape I can make. But there was forgiveness.

Here I am.

Not leaving any more.

Home.

Coda

WHEN I BEGAN THIS BOOK I had no idea how it would turn out. I was writing in real time. I was writing the past and discovering the future.

I did not know how I would feel about finding my mother. I still don't. I do know that the TV-style reunions and pink mists of happiness are wrong. We need better stories for the stories around adoption.

Many people who find their birth families are disappointed. Many regret it. Many others do not search because they feel afraid of what they might find. They are afraid of what they might feel – or worse, what they might not feel.

I met Ann again, in Manchester, just the two of us for lunch. I was glad to see her. She has my quick walk and she looks about her the way a dog does, bright, alert, and also watchful. That's me too.

She told me a bit more about my father. He wanted to keep me. She said, 'I wouldn't let him keep you. We were poor but we had floorboards.'

I love that and it makes me laugh.

Then she tells me that she used to work in a factory nearby. It was called Raffles, run by Jews, and it made the overcoats and gaberdines for Marks and Spencer. 'In those days it was all British-made, and the quality was something.'

She tells me everyone, poor or not, floorboards or not, had made-to-measure clothes, because there were so many sewing shops, and cloth was cheap. Manchester was still King of Cloth.

Her boss, Old Man Raffles, found her the mother and baby home and promised her a job when she came out.

I find that story very curious because I have always felt at home among the Jews and have a lot of Jewish friends.

'I brought you into Manchester to show you round and have your photo taken when you were three weeks old. That's the photo I sent you.'

Yes, the baby with the 'oh no don't do it' face.

I don't remember but in truth we remember everything.

There is a lot Ann can't remember. Memory loss is one way of coping with damage. Me, I go to sleep. If I am upset I can be asleep in seconds. I must have learned that myself as a Mrs Winterson survival strategy. I know I slept on the doorstep and in the coal-hole. Ann says she has never been a good sleeper.

At the end of lunch I am ready to leave or I will fall asleep right there and then at the table. Not from boredom. On the train I fall asleep at once. So there is a lot going on that I don't understand yet.

I think Ann finds me hard to read.

I think she would like me to let her be my mother. I think she would like me to be in touch regularly. But whatever adoption is, it isn't an instant family – not with the adoptive parents, and not with the rediscovered parents.

And I grew up like in all those Dickens novels, where the real families are the pretend ones; the people who become your family through deep bonds of affection and the continuity of time.

She looks at me so closely when we part.

I am warm but I am wary.

What is making me wary? What am I wary of? I don't know.

There is a big gap between our lives. She is upset about Winterson-world. She blames herself and she blames Mrs Winterson. Yet I would rather be this me – the me that I have become – than the me I might have become without books, without education, and without all the things that have happened to me along the way, including Mrs W. I think I am lucky.

How do you say that without dismissing or under-valuing things for her?

And I don't know what I feel about her. I panic when my feelings are not clear. It is like staring into a muddy pond, and rather than wait until an ecosystem develops to clear the water, I prefer to drain the pond.

This isn't a head/heart split or a thinking/feeling split. It is emotional matrix. I can juggle different and opposing ideas and realities easily. But I hate feeling more than one thing at once.

Adoption is so many things at once. And it is every-thing and nothing. Ann is my mother. She is also someone I don't know at all.

I am trying to avoid the miserable binary of 'this means so much to me/this means nothing to me'. I am trying to respect my own complexity. I had to know the story of my beginnings but I have to accept that this is a version too. It is a true story but it is still a version.

I know that Ann and Linda want to include me in their family; that is their generosity. I don't want to be included; that is not my hard-heartedness. I am so glad to know that Ann survived and I like thinking of her surrounded by the others. But I don't want to be there. That's not what's important to me. And I don't feel a biological connection. I don't feel, 'Wow, here's my mother.'

I have read a lot of overwhelmingly emotional accounts of reunion. None of that is my experience. All I can say is that I am pleased – that is the right word – that my mother is safe.

I can't be the daughter she wants.

I couldn't be the daughter Mrs Winterson wanted.

My friends who are not adopted tell me not to worry. They don't feel they were 'right' either.

I am interested in nature/nurture. I notice that I hate Ann criticising Mrs Winterson. She was a monster but she was my monster.

Ann came to London. That was a mistake. It is our third meeting and we have a serious row. I am shouting at her, 'At least Mrs Winterson was there. Where were you?'

I don't blame her and I am glad she made the choice she made. Clearly I am furious about it too.

I have to hold these things together and feel them both/all.

As a young woman Ann wasn't given much love.

'Mam didn't have time to be soft. She loved us by feeding us and clothing us.'

When her own mother was exceedingly old Ann found the courage to ask the question, 'Mam, did you love me?' Her mother was very clear. 'Yes. I love you. Now don't ask me again.'

Love. The difficult word. Where everything starts, where we always return. Love. Love's lack. The possibility of love.

I have no idea what happens next.

IN CONVERSATION:
Jeanette Winterson talks to A.M. Homes

'I never wanted to believe in the gender thing – I thought women could write anything – but now I think there's a conspiracy of small books.'

A.M. Homes was a friend before I met her, in the way that writers you sit with often become friends. The solitary act of reading is a connection. It is intimate and exposing. The writer uncovers something for you. In the silence of reading so much is said.

I read her short story debut, *The Safety of Objects*, in 1990. I was thirty, excited about finding contemporary women writers, eager to build the personal private library I needed – as a woman, as a reader, and as a writer. Men have been writing about women forever. Here was a woman writing dangerously, provocatively, about boys and men, and using the male persona. That was intriguing.

JW: Why do you write from the male perspective nearly all the time?

A.M.H.: That is my imagination. It's the place I go. I am comfortable there so I can be uncomfortable there. I find it harder, self-consciously so, to write a female narrator.

JW: How do men feel about what you do?

A.M.H.: It's interesting – I think I have a lot of male readers (I have no way to know for sure but I like to think I do). Often the letters I get are from men, and they come to the readings. I have male students in my classes. Not the soft romantic types – the geeky math types.

JW: Is it anything to do with you wanting to get away from the stereotype of women's topics, women's books? Like J.K. Rowling, you use your initials – she was told to do it otherwise boys wouldn't read her.

A.M.H.: I just don't think I can be called Amy. Do I look like an Amy? Do I write like an Amy? If I were called Jonathan, it would be easier – given the kind of things I write. We judge the content of what men and women write very differently. A lot of women get mad at me because of the violence. Maybe they never turn on the TV.

I met A.M. Homes just a few years ago in New York City where she lives with her young daughter, Juliet, and their dog Lulu. I have had good times with the kid and the dog, and long talks about everything with A.M.. We are both adopted, and that – as A.M. puts it – is a cellular unsettling that we share.

Her memoir, *The Mistress's Daughter*, is the story of her biological parents coming to find her. When I was writing *Why Be Happy When You Could Be Normal?* – my own adoption story about going to find my mother – A.M. warned me that cells have a memory. She said: "You are disturbing the deepest thing in you. It's like a raid on your DNA."

The frightening, unquantifiable, unnameable feelings are a writer's territory, but living them in your own body is like Dr. Jekyll drinking the powder and risking becoming Hyde.

We talked on a train going to Manchester where A.M. was speaking about her new book, *May We Be Forgiven,* a novel of second chances. It's a story of two hostile brothers – the age-old motif that starts with Cain and Abel. In the Homes version, beginning at Thanksgiving with ghastly family tensions splitting at the seams, Harry sleeps with George's wife Jane. George murders Jane. George goes to prison. The children are left behind. Harry takes care of them as his own marriage disappears. He comes to love them and to learn about himself. The sex and the violence in the story, the humor, the tenderness, sit around a subplot about Nixon and America and the psychosis of the American dream.

A.M.H.: If Kennedy hadn't been shot we would never have had LBJ, and without Johnson, Nixon wouldn't have happened. I am fascinated by the swerves, the chances, but also the inevitability. You look at the line of presidents, America does get what reflects it – it becomes self-explanatory.

JW: Did you deliberately polarize the two brothers Harry and George? Are they Kennedy and Nixon?

A.M.H.: No, they're not. Harry is basically a good guy. George is not a good guy. George is a high-earning executive asshole. Harry is softer, not a hero, flawed or otherwise, but a guy who has to get through the days, the nights.

JW: Toward that better version of the self.

A.M.H.: It's a novel about America now. The history part is how we got here. I didn't expect the reviews in the U.S. to be hostile. Even the good ones are somewhat hostile. It's like – she shouldn't write this stuff.

JW: Is it a gender thing?

A.M.H.: You have a better attitude here in the UK I think. Serious women writers have a better time – and they can be funny. I seem to have got into trouble in the U.S. for writing a big book, a funny book, a violent book. A book about sex. And race. A book about politics.

JW: You shouldn't have thrown it all in together. The Great American Novel has to be by Tom Wolfe or Philip Roth doesn't it?

A.M.H.: I never wanted to believe in the gender thing – I thought women could write anything – but now I think there's a conspiracy of small books. Thin books, simple books, girly books. That's fine, but I don't want to write those books.

JW: Do women in general support you? I mean apart from the violence?

A.M.H.: Grace Paley was my teacher at Sarah Lawrence College where I studied. She was gracious and generous. But women are the worst. I get my worst reviews from women – they feel fine about saying terrible things – embarrassed that praise will make them look like feminists or something.

JW: Let's hear it for feminism. I read a piece in *GQ* recently (always a good idea to read what men are saying to each other) about men's reading habits. They read much less fiction – and of the fiction they do read, only 11% of it is written by women.

A.M.H.: Will there be any fiction at all? How do you feel about the future? Making a living as a writer?

JW: I feel like it doesn't matter how good a writer you are; *Fifty Shades* will make money. And does it matter how good a miner you are if your pit closes down? No publishing, no writers.

A.M.H.: I'm developing a series for TV about the Hamptons — it's a cross between *Desperate Housewives* and *The Grapes of Wrath*.

JW: You wrote quite a lot of *The L Word* [a TV drama series about a group of lesbian, bisexual and transgender people and their friends]. That was great.

A.M.H.: But there is always some executive in your way.... I worry about money, about health insurance – now that I have a child. If you work for TV, they pay your health insurance.

JW: Does having a child change how you write? I notice that the redemption in *May We Be Forgiven* comes through the children – the possibilities they allow.

A.M.H.: I never thought I could be a mother. I thought of adopting, but I wanted a biological echo. The nearest thing to me that isn't me. Has Juliet changed how I write? A child changes, profoundly, your own sense of who you are.

JW: If I were a man, I would have a child at this point. But I am a woman and it is too late – which sounds like regret – it's not.

A.M. is gay but describes herself more honestly as bisexual. We are both politically passionate about gay rights and equality of affection, but neither of us believe that sexuality should be the dominating fact of anyone's life. We both hate it that sexual choice can be used to define the work. In any case, most of A.M.'s characters are heterosexual – though not in any easy way.

A.M.H.: I am a paid liar. I make things up. I can't write near to me.

JW: Given that women are expected to be auto-biographical, at least your literary choices allow that escape. For myself, everything comes through what I am. But I have spent my life trying to say — don't try to read me, read my work.

A.M.H.: Are you looking forward to the teaching?

JW: Yes. It interests me that creative writing is the boom industry right at the time when publishing is tanking. A new generation will have to work out how to make a living from the maddest thing anyone can do — sit down to write.

A.M.H.: Juliet comes home from school shouting, "Mom, where are you?" I say, "Right where you left me this morning, at my desk."

JW: If the sitting down doesn't pay anymore, you can always do stand-up. Have you read A.L. Kennedy? She does stand-up. Maybe we'll just all take to the road, like troubadours and tramps.